W9-DFE-025

EVAN BAYH

From FATHER *to* SON

A PRIVATE LIFE
IN THE PUBLIC EYE

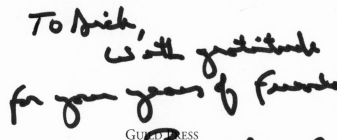

To Dick,
With gratitude
for your years of Friendship!

GUILD PRESS
EMMIS BOOKS

Evan Bayh

Copyright © 2003 by Evan Bayh

All rights reserved. No part of this book may be reproduced in any form, print or electronic, without prior written permission from the publisher. For further information, contact

GUILD PRESS / EMMIS BOOKS
40 Monument Circle
Indianapolis, Indiana 46204

ISBN 1-57860-119-3
Library of Congress Control Number 2003104224

Dust jacket design by Thrive ³, Inc.
Interior and text design by Sheila G. Samson

DUST JACKET BACK: Photo of Birch and Evan Bayh
from *Life* magazine, January 1963.

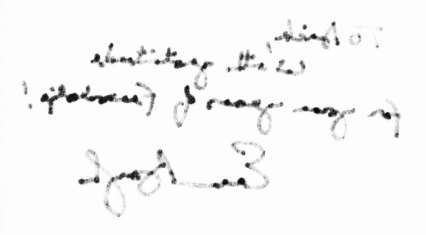

Children are the living messages we
send to a time we will not see.

—John W. Whitehead,
The Stealing of America

DEDICATION

To my wonderful sons, Beau and Nick, from your loving father—with some sound advice I received as a child courtesy of Rudyard Kipling.

IF

If you can keep your head when all about you
    Are losing theirs and blaming it on you,
If you can trust yourself when all men doubt you
    But make allowance for their doubting too,
If you can wait and not be tired by waiting,
    Or being lied about, don't deal in lies,
Or being hated, don't give way to hating,
    And yet don't look too good, nor talk too wise:

If you can dream—and not make dreams your master,
    If you can think—and not make thoughts your
        aim;
If you can meet with Triumph and Disaster
    And treat those two imposters just the same;
If you can bear to hear the truth you've spoken
    Twisted by knaves to make a trap for fools,
Or watch the things you gave your life to, broken,
    And stoop and build 'em up with worn-out tools:

If you can make one heap of all your winnings
    And risk it all on one turn of pitch-and-toss,
And lose, and start again at your beginnings
    And never breathe a word about your loss;
If you can force your heart and nerve and sinew
    To serve your turn long after they are gone,
And so hold on when there is nothing in you
    Except the Will which says to them: "Hold on!"

If you can talk with crowds and keep your virtue,
    Or walk with kings—nor lose the common touch,
If neither foes nor loving friends can hurt you;
    If all men count with you, but none to much,
If you can fill the unforgiving minute
    With sixty seconds' worth of distance run,
Yours is the Earth and everything that's in it,
    And—which is more—you'll be a Man, my son!

—Rudyard Kipling

CONTENTS

ACKNOWLEDGMENTS

Politics, like so many other things in life, is a team sport. You don't accomplish anything by yourself. Without the support of my family, good friends, my wonderful staff, and a host of volunteers, I wouldn't have been elected dogcatcher. Nor would I have been able to write this book.

Since I became involved with fatherhood issues, I've had the pleasure of meeting a number of wonderful people, national leaders of the fatherhood movement who've inspired me and taught me a great deal—Roland Warren, Wade Horn, Don Eberly, Joe Jones, and Ron Mincy—and fatherhood leaders in my home state, including Congresswoman Julia Carson, Wallace McLaughlin, and Tony and Linda Wallace of Indianapolis.

My colleagues at the Democratic Leadership Council are a constant source of ideas and support: Al From, Will Marshall, and Bruce Reed. I'm also indebted to the original cosponsors of The Responsible Fatherhood Act: Senators Pete Domenici, Richard Lugar, Joe Lieberman, Mary Landrieu, Blanche Lincoln, Chuck Robb, George Voinovich, Jeff Bingaman, and Bob Graham.

I offer a special thanks to the members of my staff who helped make this book possible—Tom Sugar, Sohini Gupta, Mark Kornblau, and Clare Glynn—as well as former staff members, Cheryl Sullivan, Joan Smith, and Richard Gordon. And to Will Allison, who helped turn my thoughts and life experiences into words on paper.

Most of all, I'd like to thank my family and close friends Carol and Bob Breshears, Gladys Sperling, Jane Sinnenberg, my mother and father, and Susan—without whom fatherhood would be only an abstraction.

FOREWORD

I first met Senator Evan Bayh on a rainy June day in 2001, at the launch of the Indiana Fatherhood Initiative. Still relatively new in my role as president of the National Fatherhood Initiative, I joined Evan on a platform in the atrium of the Children's Museum of Indianapolis to discuss the particulars of the new project. As the senator approached the podium to talk about the importance of this work for the families of Indiana, I surveyed the crowd and noticed an unusually large number of reporters and TV cameras in the audience, which filled the atrium's floor and balcony. I soon found out why: that morning, *The Indianapolis Star* had reported Evan's decision not to enter the 2004 presidential race. As he began to discuss his reasons for not running, I caught my first glimpse of the remarkable man behind the politician. Being a member of the First Family was not nearly so important to Evan as putting his family first.

As he spoke eloquently and affectionately about his five-year-old twin sons, Nicky and Beau, I saw a man who had an intimate understanding of the importance of "first things first." He recognized the coming years as pivotal in his young sons' lives. They would soon begin to ask questions that a father needs to be there to answer. They would soon start elementary school, get involved in sports, and pick up new hobbies. Evan knew that during these crucial years, being a good father to his children held much more significance than being a good president for our country.

And as he continued to speak, I noticed that he did not read from prepared remarks as elected officials almost invariably do on such occasions. He simply spoke from his heart. Convincing a group of people that involved fathers are essential to the well-being of children and society required no rehearsal on his part. This public servant's private life inspires his decision-making and shapes the things he fights for in the public arena.

In reflecting on Evan's speech that day, I realized that he spoke about issues that more Americans should understand and embrace. His most poignant remarks underscored this important truth: the essence of fatherhood is other-centeredness. Senator Bayh, a man on the brink of great power and prominence—that seductive duo that causes many to forget the things that are truly important— knew that the pursuit of such desires often means that family takes second place to reporters, cameras, a campaign staff, and a harsh political struggle. As a man who understands the important role of a dad, he chose not to take this path.

Evan also communicated values in his speech. As he stood on the podium talking about the new Indiana Fatherhood Initiative, he passionately rallied the crowd with these heartfelt assertions: We must value our families. We must value the importance of responsible fatherhood. We must value the idea that our children should have top priority in every decision that we make, both publicly and privately.

Finally, Evan emphasized the urgent need for our culture to respond to the millions of American children who have a hole in their souls in the shape of their dads. A staggering one out of three children in the United States—twenty-four million of them—grow up without a father in the home. These children are more likely to use drugs, be abused, commit crimes, live in poverty, become teen parents, and experience behavioral, health, and emotional problems.

From his speech that day, it was clear that Evan is deeply concerned about this hole that pierces the souls of so many of our nation's children. In raising his sons, he must have recognized how hard, unfair, and painful it would have been if they had to grow up without his full focus during their formative years.

That is why he stood on that stage with me that day. He was doing his part to see that as many American children as possible have the love and nurturance of their father—like the love and nurturance that he provides for his own sons. And that is why he continues, to this day, to be one of the nation's leading proponents of fatherhood initiatives. As governor and now in the Senate, he has led efforts to make revolutionary changes to the welfare system. He has fought to bring responsible fatherhood legislation to Congress, as well as legislation to reduce teen pregnancies. He recently served as a cochair of the National Fatherhood Initiative's National Summits on Fatherhood, and he currently serves as a cochair of the bipartisan Senate Task Force on Responsible Fatherhood.

In bringing sorely needed attention and resources to this issue, Evan realizes there is still work to be done, and he has not slowed his pace. The efforts to reform the welfare system continue, and, once again, Senator Bayh is on the front lines proposing innovative solutions. He is working with his colleagues on both sides of the aisle to bring a fatherhood bill to the floor, so that progress can be made in the fight against father absence. And he is doing so with the same passion and conviction that he showed at the podium when we launched the Indiana Fatherhood Initiative two years ago.

Senator Bayh's words and actions have served as a clarion call to our culture to understand the importance of responsible fatherhood. Through his example of putting first things first in his own life, he is one of the most committed and consistent voices in our nation's battle against the most pressing social problem of our times—widespread father absence. As you read the wonderful story that unfolds on the following pages, you will discover, as I have, how fortunate our nation is to have this servant-leader, Senator Evan Bayh. After all, the truest measure of a man is not what he does for himself, but what he does for others.

Roland C. Warren
President, National
    Fatherhood Initiative
Gaithersburg, Maryland
www.fatherhood.org

INTRODUCTION

I always knew that I wanted to have children someday, but until the birth of my twin sons in 1995, parenthood was an abstract idea. That all changed when I first held Nick and Beau in my arms. I'll never forget the overwhelming feeling of joy and the profound sense of responsibility I felt that day—a responsibility to do right by my sons, to protect and nurture them, to give them the best upbringing I possibly could.

Though I didn't know it at the time, that day also marked the birth of one of my greatest political passions: battling our country's epidemic of fatherlessness. I was in my second term as governor of Indiana when the twins were born, and though I'd been working for years to address problems such as teen pregnancy, educational underperformance, and crime, I was only just beginning to realize these were symptoms of a deeper underlying problem: the great number of American families in which no father is present.

Father absence was just starting to work its way into the public consciousness in 1995. The year before, the National Fatherhood Initiative was founded, and the First National Summit on Fatherhood was convened in Dallas, Texas. Two landmark books pulled together vast bodies of research that chronicled the devastating effects of father absence and fueled the growing fatherhood movement: David Blankenhorn's *Fatherless America*, and David Popenoe's *Life Without Fathers: Compelling New Evidence that Fatherhood and Marriage Are Indispensable for the Good of Children and Society.*

As I see it, one of the most profound challenges confronting our nation in the last half of the twentieth century has been the transformation of our family structure and the change in our attitudes toward raising children. Each night, more than seventeen million kids in the United States go to bed in homes without fathers. Today we lead the world in the percentage of father absence, up 300 percent from just forty years ago. Too many men are bringing children into the world and then just walking away, leaving mothers and taxpayers to pick up the pieces and the bill.

Consider the statistics: Children who aren't in contact with their fathers are five times more likely to live in poverty and ten times more likely to live in extreme poverty. They're more likely to bring weapons and drugs into the classroom. Children without fathers are twice as likely to commit crimes and drop out of school. They're more than twice as likely to abuse drugs and alcohol. Children without fathers are also more likely to commit suicide and to become teenage parents. The overwhelming majority of violent criminals—including 72 percent of adolescent murderers and 70 percent of long-term prison inmates—are males who grew up without fathers.

The rise in father absence has been accompanied by a fundamental shift in the way our society views fathers. At one end of the spectrum, the rise of two-income families has meant that fathers are more essential than ever, looked to as caregivers in addition to breadwinners. But in sharp contrast, too many men—particularly young men—view their role as fathers as superfluous, unimportant to the well-being of their children.

The increase of father absence has been mirrored by the decline of marriage. Overall, one-third of all children in the United States are born out of wedlock. The problem is more pronounced among the poor and African Americans, but it cuts across lines of race and class. It's a problem for all of us.

Researchers point to a number of reasons for the retreat from marriage, some positive, some not. First, over the past forty years, we've seen increased equality of opportunity for women, and many have entered the workforce. As women have become less financially dependent on men, however, men have unfortunately become more willing to leave the mothers of their children to fend for themselves. Second, the expansion of welfare programs in the 1960s and 1970s strengthened America's socioeconomic safety net. But by providing benefits to single parents—usually women—the welfare system created a disincentive for those parents to get married or stay married. Third, we've undergone a major revolution in cultural and sexual values in the past few decades. Our society as a whole is more tolerant of sex outside of marriage and out-of-wedlock births. Finally, the decline of marriage is also self-perpetuating. Many of today's parents are themselves products of single-parent homes and thus may place less value on marriage. These parents also lack the experience of having grown up in a married household where they could witness the kind of dedication and compromise needed to make a marriage work.

In the years since Nick and Beau were born, my sense of personal responsibility to my sons has fueled my commitment to helping all of America's children by fighting father absence in the public-policy arena. In my final year as governor, I launched an ad campaign to increase awareness of the problem, instituted a grant program to fund efforts to combat father absence, and organized a fatherhood summit in Indianapolis that brought together nearly one thousand practitioners from across the country. As a United States senator, I've promoted similar efforts at the national level and sought to shape a second generation of welfare reform that focuses on fathers. Mothers—especially single mothers—have been heroic in their efforts to raise our nation's children, but they should not be expected to shoulder the entire burden alone.

Throughout my life, I have been blessed to be surrounded by talented, strong, independent women. My mother was one. She lived on the cusp of a transitional generation that only began to enjoy the benefits of greater opportunity regardless of gender. In another time, she might have been a governor or senator. As it was, her life exemplified how our nation for too long—like some others still today—could not fulfill its full potential because half our population could not fulfill its own. Thankfully, times have changed.

My wife is a talented professional and loving mother. She works tirelessly to balance the demands of career and home, selflessly sacrificing her own interests to better help the rest of us. From her I have learned firsthand the virtues of patience, kindness, wisdom, and love that mothers, married or single, bring to the cause of raising healthy, well-adjusted children.

As an avid reader of military history, I have read countless accounts of soldiers grievously wounded in battle, crying out in pain and despair—always for their mothers. Clearly, mothers bring something unique and indispensable to the process of making us who we are. But fathers offer something positive and special too, something that today is too often lost.

Sadly, the epidemic of father absence continues largely unchecked, yet on Capitol Hill we're still spending billions of dollars each year to deal with its symptoms rather than tackling the root cause. This book is the story of my life, as a son, as a father, and as an advocate of responsible fatherhood. It's my hope that this will help bring attention to the issue of father absence and encourage America to get serious about meeting this challenge so that one day all of our children can grow up in loving, nurturing homes that offer them the best chance to make the most of their God-given abilities.

Evan Bayh
March 2003

1

MY SONS ARRIVE

The whole situation was surreal, being there with Susan in real time and watching the news reports almost simultaneously.

BECAUSE MY FATHER and I both chose careers in politics, Election Day has always been an important time in my family. Still, no Election Day prepared me for November 7, 1995. I was working in my office at the state capitol that Tuesday morning when I got a call from my wife, Susan, telling me that her doctor had decided to induce labor. It took a minute for what she was saying to sink in: I was about to become a father. I'd known for months that my life would soon change forever, but I wasn't sure exactly how. Were we ready for this? Could we handle it? Would I be a good father? I took a deep breath, just like I'd been doing all along, and told myself everything would be fine. Having children is an act of faith as much as anything else.

We arranged to meet at St. Vincent Hospital, and before Susan hung up, she rattled off a quick list of clothes and other items for me to pick up at the governor's residence. After I swung by the house, I also couldn't help stopping along the way to vote. I guess it's just in my blood. Even so, I was only going through the motions as I stepped up to the voting machine that morning. My thoughts were with Susan, the miscarriage she'd had two years earlier, the hard times we'd been through. I was praying things would work out this time.

In 1993, when a reporter learned that Susan was pregnant and insisted on running the story, we decided to hold a press conference so that we could share the news on our own terms. One week after we made the announcement, Susan had the miscarriage. Not everyone heard the bad news, though, and for the next several months, people kept asking us, "When is the baby due? How's the baby?" We didn't want to risk the pain of another public miscarriage, so when Susan got pregnant with the twins, we waited sixteen weeks before we went public with the news. We knew from the sonogram that one of the twins was smaller than the other, and we wanted to be sure they'd both make it. Now, twenty weeks later, all that remained was the labor and delivery. However, we were still in for a much longer haul than we expected.

I was the first governor of Indiana since 1830 to become a father while in office, so it was not only a new experience for us, but for everybody else in the state as well. From the moment I arrived at the hospital at 11:45 A.M., it felt as if the whole state was watching. The media attention and the public interest were natural and well-intentioned, just another example of a public official's life in a fishbowl. I had to come in through the hospital's back delivery entrance. Four satellite trucks were already parked out front, and reporters had even tried to get into Susan's room, but the state police kept them out.

Aside from the media attention—and aside from the fact that we had twins—our experiences at the hospital weren't so different from those of many other parents, but for me, that day and the days that followed were a revelation.

The doctor induced labor shortly after I arrived, and Susan was officially in labor by 1 P.M. The TV stations broke into their news broadcasts for live updates on her status, reporting the details of her dilation and contractions. She gazed up at the TV, a little shocked.

"Come on," I said. "It's not so bad."

"It's not *your* body," she said.

The reporters were eager to speak with Susan's doctor, Madalyn Squires, and Susan encouraged her to do an interview. "It will be good for your practice."

"Number one," Madalyn said, "I don't really need any more patients. Number two, you're in labor. Shouldn't I be here with you?"

Susan managed a smile in between contractions. "I knew there was a reason I picked you."

The whole situation was surreal, being there with Susan in real time and watching the news reports almost simultaneously. Tom Sugar, who was my communications director then and is now my chief of staff, was going back and forth between the delivery room and the press area. We'd tell him how the labor was progressing, he'd go update the reporters, and by the time he came back, they'd be on TV reporting what he just told them. It wasn't long, though, before the news coverage became background noise, part of the scenery. Susan and I were too focused on the labor to notice much else.

Susan was still in labor when her mother, Carol, arrived that evening. Susan had called her mom as soon as Dr. Squires decided to induce labor. Carol lives in Los Angeles, and she was on the freeway when she got Susan's call. She promptly turned around, drove straight to the airport, and caught the first flight to Indianapolis.

Carol was pretty hungry by the time she arrived, and so was I. From the window of Susan's room, we could see the sign for

Shapiro's Deli, one of my favorite restaurants. The temptation was too much; Carol ran out to get us dinner. When she returned and unwrapped two mouth-watering pastrami sandwiches, poor Susan could only sit and watch: for eight months the doctors had her eating for three, but now that she was in labor, she wasn't allowed to eat anything but ice chips. Sheepish at my insensitivity, I promised her a meal fit for a king as soon as the doctor would allow.

I spent the night in a chair beside Susan's bed, dozing for perhaps an hour. The labor stretched on through the morning and into the afternoon. Finally, after Susan had endured twenty-six grueling hours, Dr. Squires decided to abandon natural childbirth in favor of a C-section.

Susan didn't hesitate. "Okay," she said. "I'm ready to go."

They wheeled her down the hall to an operating room, and I put on hospital scrubs while they prepared her for surgery. The C-section came off without a hitch. Susan was the portrait of calm and courage, never worrying about the spinal tap or anything else. I managed to control my nerves through the delivery and took plenty of pictures.

The doctor delivered Beau first, at 3:06 P.M., and held him up for us to see. "You have a healthy baby . . . son!" Until that moment, we hadn't known whether the babies were boys or girls.

"He's so beautiful," Susan said.

Then the doctor went back to work. About a minute later, she delivered Nick. "And he has a healthy baby . . . brother!"

Susan turned to me. "Three men in the family—I'm going to have my hands full!" How prophetic she was.

Beau's full name is Birch Evans Bayh IV. Nick's full name is Nicholas Harrison Bayh. Harrison comes from President William Henry Harrison, a distant relation on my father's side of the family. We didn't want Nick to feel slighted because he didn't inherit my name, so we tell him, "Nick, you're named for a president. Beau's only named for a senator."

Considering they were born four weeks early, both boys were fairly large: Beau weighed five pounds, fourteen ounces and measured eighteen and three-quarters inches; Nick was even bigger at six pounds, two ounces, and twenty and one-quarter inches. The doctors checked their vitals and both boys scored nine out of ten on the APGAR test. The long labor had made me a little goofy: I joked that we'd have to include those scores on the boys' college applications.

As soon as the doctors finished examining the boys, I got to hold them, first one and then the other. That was among the most remarkable moments in my life. There's no way to describe it other than to say that it was emotionally overwhelming. I remember rocking each of them in my arms, gazing into their eyes. I kept telling them over and over, "Your daddy loves you very much." That's the one thing I wanted them to know more than anything else.

A couple hours after the boys were born, I went out to face the press with a box of blue bubble-gum cigars. Passersby were congratulating me in the hallway. I was still wearing my hospital smock and pants, a surgical mask around my neck. I'd hardly slept at all since I woke up Tuesday morning, but I was sailing along, running on adrenaline. I was thirty-nine years old; this was the happiest day of my life.

The press conference aired on live TV for fifteen or twenty minutes, which is a long time for television. The stations also showed parts of the interview on the evening news, with the boys practically edging out the election coverage. Even today, people tell me they remember the hospital press conference; they say it made them feel like they were reliving the birth of their own children. And ever since that day, people in Indiana ask me about the twins more than anything else.

After I finished talking with the reporters, Susan and I went to the recovery room while the nurses took the boys to the nursery to clean them up. By then, phone calls were pouring into the hospital—more than two hundred in all, including one from President Clinton—but the only person I spoke with in those first few hours was my father. We made plans for him to come to Indianapolis the following week. Later that night, Susan and I spoke with other callers, including Ethel Kennedy, the widow of Robert F. Kennedy and the mother of Robert Kennedy, Jr., who'd been a classmate of mine in law school.

At the Democratic Party state headquarters, they'd started getting calls on Tuesday afternoon. Usually when people call party headquarters on Election Day, they want to know where to vote; this year, they were calling to ask if the twins had been born. On Wednesday, the staff at party headquarters also fielded calls from well-wishers including Jimmy Carter and Christopher Dodd, chairman of the Democratic National Committee.

Waiting in the recovery room, Susan and I were eager to see the boys again. Finally, the nurses rolled them in, each in his own little crib. That's when I nearly panicked.

"Whoa!" I said. "I think there may be a problem here."

"What's that?" the nurse said.

I pointed to the nametags on the cribs. They were supposed to say "Bayh baby." Instead, they said "Stein baby." I thought our boys had gotten mixed up with someone else's.

As it turns out, the state police had instructed the hospital to assign aliases to the boys for security reasons. (On a subsequent trip to the nursery, Nick and Beau became the "Hamilton babies.") Somebody had phoned in threats to the hospital. The police were unable to rule out the possibility that the calls had come from inside the building, but they did their usual good job handling the situation. The only problem came weeks later, when we began receiving hospital bills for the Stein and Hamilton babies.

Usually twins have to sleep in the preemie nursery, but Beau and Nick were big enough that they were allowed to stay in Susan's room where she could nurse them. The reporters wanted us to hold a press conference with the boys there in the recovery room, but Susan nixed that idea. She was pretty exhausted and not feeling her most photogenic. For starters, she hadn't washed her hair in three days. "One camera, one reporter, and I get to pick 'em," she said. She chose a photographer from *The Indianapolis Star*, and before the photographer arrived, she had a hair stylist come to her room. He washed her hair in a trash can because she wasn't allowed to shower or take a bath so soon after surgery. A photo of us and the kids ran on the front page of Friday's paper—Susan in bed, me by her side, each of us holding a twin. They were swaddled in handmade blankets that had been sent to them by Sister Laura Gall of the Sisters of St. Joseph of Tipton.

In the coming days, we received dozens of bouquets, cards, toys, and stuffed animals (including a couple of GOP elephants from Republican state chairman Mike McDaniel). The people of Indiana could not have been nicer to us. Many of the gifts we passed along to less fortunate children, but we did keep a few. To this day, each of the boys still has a "blankie" with his name stitched on it. They also fell in love with a couple of stuffed dogs they received from golf course designers Pete and Alice Dye. The "woofies," as they came to be known, were among the most modest of their stuffed animals, but Nick and Beau took a fierce liking to them and for years wouldn't sleep without them. Now that the boys are older, they aren't quite so attached to their woofies, but early on, the misplacement of a woofie constituted a major family crisis.

A few days after the boys were born, we brought them home from the hospital to 4750 North Meridian Street, a house that became the governor's residence in 1975. Nick and Beau were the first children to live at that governor's residence. The previous governor's residence at 4343 Meridian had last seen children during the term of Edgar Whitcomb, who moved in with his five kids in 1969. That house had also been home to the nineteen-year-old twin daughters of Governor Matt Welsh, who took office in 1961 and was instrumental in helping my father secure the Democratic nomination for Senate in 1962.

The governor's residence is where Nick and Beau would spend the first fourteen months of their lives. It's where they were living when they were christened by Reverend Nancy Ferriani in a wonderful ceremony at Trinity Episcopal Church. It's where they learned how to lift their heads, roll over, and crawl. It's where they took their first steps and said their first word, which I'm happy to report was "Da-da." The governor's residence is also where Susan and I learned about changing diapers, feeding infants, deciphering their various cries, and coaxing them to sleep. As an only child who'd never cared for younger siblings, I found the experience eye-opening and humbling, to say the least.

The staff at the governor's residence was very helpful and understanding as Susan and I set about transforming the house to accommodate the boys. In those days, the staff consisted of house manager Lyle Browne; Thelma and Rose, who handled the upkeep and cleaning; Dexter, who did maintenance; and security guards, whose office was located in the basement. The previous first family also had a butler and a cook, but Susan and I felt more comfortable in a less formal household.

Next to the master bedroom upstairs was a sitting parlor, which we converted into a nursery for the boys. Susan put up wallpaper with a frieze along the top that pictured cows jumping over the moon. The boys slept in matching cribs with matching mobiles, and they received their seemingly unending 2 A.M. feedings in the rocking chair between the cribs. Across the hall on the back side of the house was a second bedroom where we kept their high chairs and set up a play area. Once they were ready for solid food, we'd heat up their meals in the kitchen downstairs, then come up the back staircase. I always enjoyed feeding them—"Here comes the airplane, open up the hangar!"—and I considered the meal a success whenever I got more *in* the boy than *on* the boy. That second bedroom was spacious and carpeted, and in later months that's where the boys practiced crawling.

These days, when people mention to me that they're having a baby, I tell them to get ready for big changes. Like movies? Watch them now. Like going out to dinner with your spouse? Go now. Like to sleep? Sleep now. Of course, our experience was more intense because we had two babies instead of one. When the going got rough, I couldn't say to Susan, "Honey, I'm exhausted. Can you hold the baby?" because the answer would be, "What do you mean? I'm *already* holding a baby."

The boys are fraternal, not identical, twins, and we quickly realized they had very distinct personalities. At any given time during their early childhood, they weren't necessarily on the same sleeping schedule, eating schedule, diaper schedule, or developmental schedule. Nick, who is more cautious, crawled backward before he crawled forward and took his time learning to walk. Beau, who in those days was more physical, basically threw himself at targets throughout the house. At their first birthday party, he even threw himself facedown in the cake.

The first eight months were a blur. At first, I was nervous around the boys and treated them as if they were made of porcelain. When they cried I'd try to calm them down and would end up making them cry more. I'd show up at the statehouse with spit-up on my shoulder and not even know it. One of the good things about being governor is that you're in the state most of the time, as opposed to being a senator, which requires more national and international travel. I could visit three or four cities around the state in one day and still make it home at night. Being governor is a twenty-four-hours-a-day, seven-days-a-week job, just like parenthood, so I was never really off the clock.

But it was Susan who did most of the parenting work, especially since she was breastfeeding. Fortunately, we had some help. After we brought the boys home from the hospital, Susan's mom stayed with us for several days, as did Jane Sinnenberg, who'd been my mother's best friend and has become a surrogate grandmother to the boys. Right after the grandmothers left, we hired a nurse, a wonderful woman named Otrivia See, who'd been one of our delivery-room nurses. For a month or so, she'd come over at eleven o'clock and stay until six in the morning. You could tell she worked with babies all day. She'd pick up both boys, start rocking them, and they'd be asleep in no time. I remember looking at her and thinking, "How do you do that?"

Some nights, the boys would cry in tandem for hours on end. Friends suggested taking them for a late-night car ride, but as governor, I didn't think it would be wise to cruise the city in my pajamas. Instead, I'd hold one baby and Susan would hold the other, and we'd make circuits through the house, starting in the bedroom and looping down to my office and back. One night when Beau was two or three months old, he had an adverse reaction to an inoculation and would not be calmed down. I tried walking the floors, rocking him, singing to him, but nothing worked. I was exasperated, he was exasperated. We ended up heading to the basement. I figured as long as we were going to be up all night, I'd watch TV and walk on the treadmill, but as soon as I stepped onto it, something miraculous happened: Beau stopped crying—and looked at me as if I were out of my mind. I probably was. I'd reached the point where I hardly knew what I was doing. Still, I like to think that somewhere deep down inside, Beau felt safe and secure in his father's arms.

Of course, there are always going to be times when you *can't* make your children feel safe and secure, and as a father, that's been one of the hardest facts for me to accept. Before the twins were born, the doctors did an ultrasound and discovered that each boy had a kink in his ureter, the tube that links his kidneys to his bladder—not an uncommon problem, but one that can lead to kidney damage over time. We were fortunate the doctors caught the problem so early. In the past, when technology wasn't as advanced, the condition would often go undetected until a child was four or five years old. One day the child would have an ache in his side, and the next day, he'd lose a kidney.

Beau outgrew the problem within six months or so, but Nick wasn't so lucky. Until he was one year old, he had to undergo a dye test every three months to monitor his condition. The procedure is particularly unpleasant for a boy. The doctors had to insert a catheter and inject a dye into his system, which they then viewed using an X-ray. It still breaks my heart to think of him lying there under the big X-ray machine with the catheter inside him, crying and crying. The poor little guy didn't know what was going on, and all I could do was hold his hand, stroke his head, and try to help him get through it.

When Nick was a year old, his doctor recommended surgery. He told us the procedure had a 97 percent success rate, but we still didn't like the idea of Nick going under general anesthesia at that age. We decided to get a second opinion and learned that 90 percent of kids eventually outgrow the problem and that many parents were adopting a wait-and-see approach in lieu of surgery. These days, Nick still has to get checked out once a year, but it looks as if his condition is slowly resolving itself, which is a blessing and a big relief. Susan and I know how fortunate we are to have two healthy sons. So many things can go wrong with children, and so much of it is out of your control.

2
THE KEYNOTE SPEECH

*Once I got up on the podium, it was clear to me
within seconds that the setting was a disaster, that no
one was paying attention, and that there was nothing
I could do except plow ahead.*

THE FIRST TIME I was faced with a political decision that affected
my sons came when I was invited to give the keynote speech at the
1996 Democratic National Convention and had to choose whether
or not I wanted the boys to be involved. That August, during my
final months as governor, we took a family vacation to Bermuda.
The boys were about nine months old, and this was their first visit
to the ocean. While we were there, President Clinton called to ask if
I'd give the main speech in Chicago later that month.

It was a phone call I'd been hoping for. Earlier that summer, I'd
been contacted by Bob Squier, a close advisor to President Clinton
and Vice President Gore who'd handled television advertising both
for me and for Clinton's reelection campaign. Bob had big news:
The president was considering me for the keynote speech. Would I
be interested? I'd told him of course I would.

The president's invitation was a tremendous honor for me and
for Indiana. No Hoosier had given the keynote speech at a party

convention since Dick Lugar, now Indiana's senior senator, addressed the Republicans in Miami back in 1972, when he was mayor of Indianapolis.

I think the president chose me for a number of reasons. For starters, I'm viewed as a moderate with a record of attracting independent and Republican voters as well as Democrats. I was Indiana's first Democratic governor in twenty years, and no Democrat had carried the state in a presidential race since Lyndon Johnson in 1964. Also, I'm from the Midwest, a key battleground in national elections. My youth probably helped, too. I was forty at the time. When I'd first been elected eight years earlier, at age thirty-two, I was the youngest governor in the country, a title once held by Bill Clinton when he was governor of Arkansas. We also shared something else in common: we'd both become fathers during our time as governors.

President Clinton had met Nick and Beau earlier that year when Susan and I took them on their very first trip, a New Year's visit to Hilton Head, South Carolina. We were there for the annual Renaissance Weekend, a nonpolitical, nonpartisan family retreat for leaders in a wide range of fields. The Renaissance Weekends were founded in 1981 by a Hilton Head couple named Phil and Linda Lader, and what had started with sixty families now included close to five hundred families and a weekend packed with more than three hundred programs and presentations on topics ranging from arts and letters to sports, economics and investments, medical breakthroughs, science and technology, political issues, public policy, and a range of personal issues.

Susan and I attended the gathering for eight or nine years in a row, meeting lots of interesting people and making some good friends. The Clintons were regulars, too. That year, we got a great picture of the president holding the twins, one in each arm. Even though the boys were only six weeks old, Susan and I had already learned that when they cried, they usually had a good reason. If we wanted to avoid a meltdown, we couldn't just cross our fingers and hope for the best. We made sure they had a nice nap and weren't hungry. They were remarkably calm and quiet in his arms.

"Mr. President," I said, "you're a natural."

He just shook his head and laughed. "Yeah, for some reason, children, dogs, and mosquitoes—they all take a liking to me."

I was excited about giving the keynote speech, but I was also aware that it was a big responsibility and that I'd better do it well. As it was, I didn't have much time to prepare. The convention was only two or three weeks away. President Clinton was famous for putting off important decisions until the last moment, and he'd waited as long as possible to assess the political dynamic of the convention before choosing a keynote speaker.

I usually give speeches off the top of my head, working from a rough outline that I may or may not jot down. This time, though, I wrote out the speech word for word, not leaving anything to chance. Also, for the first and only time so far, I hired a speechwriter to help me, which turned out to be a rather mixed experience. Bob Squier had recommended the writer to me. He'd authored a number of successful speeches, but we didn't have a lot of time to work on this one, much less time to get a good feel for one another. As a result, he basically had to write the speech in a vacuum, so it was little surprise that it didn't end up sounding much like me. I then had to sit down and rewrite large sections of it.

The role of the keynote speech has changed over the years. Up until the last two or three conventions, its purpose was to outline the party's broad policy vision and set the tone for the convention.

It was a forum to tell the country, "Here's who we are. Here's what we stand for. If you put your trust in us, here's where we hope to lead the nation." But at recent conventions—including the 1996 convention in Chicago, where I was to speak—the speech has been less about broad themes and more specifically focused on helping the presidential nominee get elected.

Some of the president's advisors wanted me to take a negative tone, attacking Bob Dole and Newt Gingrich. I believe there's a time and a place to give hard-edged speeches, but I was reluctant to do it in this case. The president was well ahead, had many accomplishments to highlight, and the public was sick of "politics as usual"—including negative campaigning. Thankfully, the president agreed. There was no need to slash and burn. When we discussed it, he said, "Look, I didn't ask you to do this because you're a hatchet man. You've got to be true to who you are." Later, he called me from his car and went over every word of the speech with me, literally approving it line by line, suggesting changes here and there. By the end of that conversation, I was calling him the Editor in Chief instead of the Commander in Chief.

What looked like a great opportunity ended up being anything but. I arrived in Chicago with Susan and the boys the day before the convention, and my staff set up Teleprompters in the hotel room so I could practice my speech. I remember lying on the bed with the manuscript and a pen, going over last-minute changes on the phone with the president while Susan kept the boys occupied at the window, pointing out sights in the Chicago skyline.

My speech was scheduled for the second night of the convention. Susan and the boys were sitting in the audience with her mother, my father, and Jane Sinnenberg. Keeping the boys happy turned out to be a difficult task. The keynote address was slated for nine o'clock—well past their bedtime—and the program was already running late. I ended up getting pushed back to almost ten o'clock. By then, a lot of the delegates thought the convention was over for the night. About half the crowd had already left, and others were headed for the exits. To further complicate matters, the convention had run late the night before, and the TV networks had said that they were going to cut off coverage at ten o'clock sharp, no matter what. My speech was eleven or twelve minutes long. By the time I stepped onstage, it was two minutes till ten, Central Time. The organizers had planned to introduce the keynote speech by dimming the lights and showing a video about me, but there was no time for that. They basically told me to just get out there and start speaking. Since they didn't dim the lights, many of the delegates didn't even realize that the keynote speech was about to start.

Once I got up on the podium, it was clear to me within seconds that the setting was a disaster, that no one was paying attention, and that there was nothing I could do except plow ahead. I comforted myself with the memory of Bill Clinton's widely criticized speech introducing Michael Dukakis at the convention eight years earlier, a speech that ran almost forty-five minutes. When he neared the end and said, "In conclusion . . ." everybody had cheered. As I stood there talking to a half-full and rapidly emptying convention hall, I assured myself that it was possible to survive a less-than-stellar convention speech.

My speech was almost universally panned by the pundits and reviewers, partly because it didn't contain a lot of red meat—no hacking and slashing of the Republican Party, no personal attacks on Bob Dole—but mainly because of its reception within the convention hall, which wasn't as strong as I wanted it to be, either.

There was, however, a silver lining. The convention organizers had made a calculated gamble that the networks wouldn't cut off the keynote speech—and they were right. As a result, when people up and down the East Coast turned on their TVs for the local eleven o'clock news, Eastern Time, they got me instead. I ended up with a larger viewing audience than any of the previous speakers that night—a lineup that included heavy hitters such as Jesse Jackson, Mario Cuomo, and Hillary Clinton—and my speech earned the second-highest rating among viewers. The reporters who were in the hall watching the calamity unfold could see only the awful circumstances, but out there in the televised world, where you're communicating with millions of people (which is what really matters these days) the speech actually went over pretty well.

I remember walking off the stage and running into Tom Ochs, one of Bob Squier's top associates. He'd watched the speech on a TV monitor in a little room behind the podium. I was feeling about as low as I possibly could.

"That was awful," I said. "Humiliating."

"What do you mean?" Tom said.

"Are you blind?" I asked. "Didn't you just see that speech?"

He shrugged. "It looked great on TV."

"Really?"

"Yeah," he said. "It looked perfectly fine."

Hearing that was a big relief. Later, at the post-speech party, the president called to congratulate me on a job well done. I think he felt pretty bad about the extenuating circumstances, but even though the speech didn't go as well as either of us had hoped, I've never dwelled on it publicly. I don't think crying over spilled milk does much good, so I just tried to make the best of it.

After the speech, I was joined onstage by my father, Susan's mother, Susan, and the boys. Nick and Beau had appeared on television in Indiana, but this was their first time on live national TV. We stood together on the podium, waving to the crowd and feeling somewhat disoriented and odd as our image was projected onto a giant video screen directly behind us.

As soon as we walked off the stage, the boys broke down, which was no surprise since it was hours past their bedtime. I'm really glad they were there, though. During the weeks leading up to the convention, Susan and I talked a lot about whether they should come to Chicago with us. They'd been making public appearances since they were photographed in the hospital two days after they were born, but for the most part, we tried to keep them out of the spotlight.

Some people no doubt see my boys as a political asset, but that's certainly not the way I see them. That would be cynical and, frankly, a bit strange. They're our *children*. There's a fine line between parading your kids for public benefit and simply sharing important public events together as a family. People want to know who their elected officials are and what makes them tick. I think that interest is natural and appropriate to a certain point, and for me (as for most people) family is a big part of what makes me tick. So at that time, it just seemed to me the natural thing to have Nick and Beau there at the convention, considering what an important part of my life they are and what an important event it was for me. I think it would be *unnatural* to not have your family present at a major event in your life. Besides, the public is pretty smart. They can readily spot someone who is cynically manipulating his family for political benefit. We've all seen candidates who run for office under the banner of "family values" and who, it turns out, have less than unceasing fidelity to their own families. If you're genuine—if you let people know who you are and what you care about in a tactful way—I think the public recognizes and appreciates that.

3

THE NEED FOR GOOD FATHERS

The way I see it, nobody requires you to bring children into the world, but if you choose to do so, you should be committed to loving and caring for them.

I SUPPOSE BEING a father myself has made me more sensitive to the lives of children, but I have always cared about kids, especially those who haven't had the advantages many children enjoy. In fact, of all the people I've encountered during my years in public life, children have left the strongest impressions on me. I remember a little girl I met when I was touring a Head Start facility in LaPorte back in 1992. The teacher was showing me around the daycare center, introducing me to some of the kids, when this brown-haired girl in a pretty dress came over, threw her arms around my waist, and looked up at me with hopeful eyes. She was only four or five years old.

"Will you be my daddy?" she said.

Her words were like a knife in my heart. I was speechless. Something important was missing in her life—something other children had that she didn't—and she knew it. All I could do was hug her and tell her I'd be her friend. Later, I learned that she was living with her grandparents because her father had been killed in a motorcycle accident and her mother had been in and out of institutions. I ended up corresponding with her and taking her to the state fair one summer, but even during the brief time we spent together, I was no substitute for her real father.

Make no mistake about it: father absence hurts children. As governor, I'd become all too familiar with its devastating effects as we worked to address a connected web of social problems that have their roots in the breakdown of families. When I came to office in 1989, for example, the state was experiencing a corrections crisis. Fueled by an increase in drug-related convictions, the inmate population was exploding. The federal courts had limited the number of inmates we could put in our existing facilities, and the state hadn't been building prisons quickly enough, so we were faced with a shortage of prison beds. The connection between crime and the breakdown of family structures was driven home to me by Jim Aiken, head of our Department of Corrections. I'd hired Jim after conducting a national search for someone capable of turning around Indiana's prison woes. Upon taking the job, one of the first things Jim did was to confer with experts from around the country to create a model to predict the long-range rise in inmate population. The success of this model was critical, because building a new prison can take six or seven years—the state needed to get ahead of the curve and stay there.

I took a great interest in this project not only because it involved public safety, but also because penitentiaries are very expensive to both build and operate. Each inmate costs up to fifty thousand dollars a year, depending on the type of facility. I remember meeting with Jim one afternoon in my office. I asked him to explain to me how he could predict the number of criminals we'd be incarcerating in the future. Jim got a sorrowful look on his face.

"Governor, do you really want to know?"

I told him I did, but I still wasn't prepared for his answer.

"We've got this equation," he said, "and it's got a lot of variables in it. But the single most reliable predictor is the number of at-risk children in second grade today."

In other words, we look at the circumstances currently facing *eight-year-olds* in order to gauge how full our jails will be six or seven years down the road. If ever there were a powerful argument for early intervention, for ensuring that kids grow up in the best possible circumstances, this is it.

One of the hardest things I had to deal with as governor was capital punishment. After an inmate had exhausted his judicial appeals in the state and federal court systems, he'd appeal to the parole board for a pardon or clemency. The parole board would then make a recommendation and send the case to me. As governor, I had the sole power under the state constitution to grant a reprieve, a commutation, or a pardon. In my view, it was one of the most awesome responsibilities I had, because it was quite literally a matter of life and death on one hand, weighed against my obligations to the victims and society on the other.

I reviewed three death-penalty appeals during my time in office and did not see fit to grant a pardon in any of those cases. The first two stemmed from the same crime, the murder of a police officer. The third involved a brutal killing that took place on New Year's Day. The perpetrator had spent the day drinking and using drugs at a local bar. When he ran out of money, he and his buddy called a cab with the intention of robbing the driver so they'd have money to keep their party going. They instructed the driver to take them to a remote area where they not only robbed him, but forced him to strip down, bound him hand and foot, and made him beg for his life. The cab driver told the men that his wife had terminal cancer and that his children would soon be orphaned if they killed him. They shot him anyway. As it turns out, the driver was telling them the truth. His wife died shortly thereafter, and their son and daughter were split up, each sent to live with different grandparents.

Whenever a death-penalty case crossed my desk, emotions ran high—for the public, for the prisoner and his family, for me and my family. Around the time when I was reviewing one of the cases involving the murdered police officer, Susan and I took the boys for a walk in their stroller. We were headed north on Meridian, just a few blocks from the governor's residence, when a car came up the street and circled the block. As it passed, a guy leaned out the window and yelled, "Murderer!" The next time the car came around, it stopped and two men got out. They started walking toward us, and it was clear they were belligerent. I turned around and waved to the Capitol security officer who was following us in his patrol car. He pulled up and we got the kids into the car just in time. As we drove away, the two men grabbed the stroller and threw it into the street.

Of the three capital murder cases I reviewed, two sentences were carried out during my term. On the night of an execution, a direct phone line is set up connecting the governor's residence to the death chamber at the state penitentiary. I'll never forget that first night, sitting next to the phone. It was late. A couple hundred demonstrators had gathered outside the house, denouncing me as a murderer, a cold-hearted killer. I was watching the clock with the knowledge that if I didn't pick up that phone by 1 A.M.—midnight at the state prison in Michigan City—the sentence would be carried out. That's a part of the job I don't miss. After the execution, the family of the deceased pulled up in front of the governor's residence with the hearse, the dead man's body still inside. They spent about twenty minutes there, shouting and honking their horns. A few days later, somebody drove by and fired a shot at the house.

Reviewing a capital punishment case was an awesome responsibility—not quite like playing God, because only God can forgive your sins—but certainly the ultimate act of carrying out the power of society over an individual. I'll never forget reading through those files. Each one basically told a life story, and time after time, the story was the same. I could see, from a very early age, a life careening out of control: A young man gets into trouble at school, drops out, ends up in the juvenile justice system, then graduates to the adult criminal justice system. The severity of his violations gets worse and worse until finally he commits a heinous murder or multiple murder—often without remorse—and ends up on Indiana's Death Row. I would read those files and think, "My God, how does this happen?" While many factors contribute, one was almost always present: These offenders came from totally dysfunctional families. You could readily see the nexus between their early childhood experiences and their eventual violent behavior.

Consider the man who murdered the cab driver. At a very early age, he was abandoned by his birth mother, who literally threw him away. He was found in a dumpster by a passerby who heard him crying. For a while, he lived with prostitutes. He eventually landed in a foster home where he was subjected to ultra-strict discipline and frequent corporal punishment. Soon he was committing petty crimes, then more serious crimes. His life offers yet another example of how things can go horribly wrong for kids who come from disintegrated families that deny them nurturing, love, and affection. I remember thinking to myself, "This guy didn't have a chance," but at the same time, I recognized that there are other people who grow up in terribly adverse circumstances and nevertheless don't end up committing cold-blooded murder.

My administration tried to break this cycle of young lives spinning out of control by opening the state's first boot camp for juvenile offenders. It was a tough-love approach. We were trying to tell these kids, "You can't keep going down this road. You've got to turn your life around." But even though we were intervening early, before these kids ended up on Death Row, we still weren't getting at the root cause, the dysfunctional family background that started too many on the path to crime in the first place.

In the end, it's not just the kids who are the problem; parents, too, must bear responsibility for shattered lives and the impact of those lives on society. During my first year as governor, when crack was becoming a serious problem in Indiana, the state police planned a simultaneous raid on several locations in conjunction with the federal authorities and local police. In order to elevate public awareness of the drug problem and bring attention to the efforts we were making to fight drugs, I attended one of those busts, a raid on a dilapidated crack house in Michigan City. I went inside after the police had secured the area and was shocked by what I saw: a rat-infested house with human feces and rotting garbage all over the floor. Never before had I seen the human condition so degraded. Worst of all, three or four young children were there. The police had gathered them in what had once been the living room while the adults were being arrested in a dank bedroom strewn with filthy mattresses.

It's bad enough for parents to blow their minds on drugs, but it struck me as inhuman for them to subject their children to such a debased environment. What chance did those kids have? They were starting off life with two and a half strikes against them. And it's not as if they'd been born with some terrible juvenile disease; this hardship was intentionally inflicted upon them by their parents. The way I see it, nobody requires you to bring children into the world, but if you choose to do so, you should be committed to loving and caring for them. In the end, it's an issue of justice: It's not fair to make children pay the price for their parents' mistakes. Unfortunately, it happens every day.

Indiana was also experiencing an educational crisis, another problem related to the breakdown of families. Kids who don't live with their fathers are more likely to bring drugs and weapons to school, and they're twice as likely to drop out. During my first two years in office, we brought in experts from around the country and put together an education strategy for the state. Unfortunately, the recession of the early nineties created a budget crunch that forced us to focus on the economy and budgetary matters for the next couple of years. In my second term, we were finally able to enact a number of landmark educational improvements. My predecessor, Governor Bob Orr, had made significant progress in the area of education, working to reduce the size of classes and institute a system of statewide exams—what came to be known as the ISTEP tests. While we had some disagreements, I wanted to build on his work and take the state's educational system to the next level by raising academic standards, increasing accountability, and providing more funding and resources for better results. We instituted a high-school graduation test that students had to pass in order to get their diplomas, and we increased funding for both advanced-placement courses and for after-school and summer remedial programs to help students who did poorly on the ISTEPs. We also made the ISTEP examinations a more "authentic" assessment of student performance, to borrow the pedagogical term. In addition to selected-response questions, such as true-false and multiple-choice, we added constructed-response questions, such as essays. When you ask a child to read a passage and give you a written answer, you learn a lot more about what the child knows or doesn't know, how he thinks, whether he can reason, and whether he can write.

We also took a giant step in helping more Hoosiers to attend college. If I had to pick my single proudest achievement from my days as governor, it would be the Twenty-first Century Scholars Program, which we started in 1990. This program guarantees a college education to every Hoosier schoolchild of modest means who is willing to sign a pledge of good citizenship in middle school and who graduates from high school with a grade-point average of at least 2.0.

The program is open to all seventh- and eighth-graders who qualify for free or reduced-priced lunches under the national school lunch program. We picked that age group because an Indiana State University study determined that it's in seventh and eighth grade that kids first begin considering college, asking themselves whether they're college material, whether college is a realistic goal for them. We didn't want money to be the barrier that prevented any child from going to college, and we saw this program as a way of breaking the cycles of poverty and ignorance.

The citizenship pledge requires the children to not experiment with drugs or alcohol and to stay out of trouble with the law. At least one parent must sign the pledge, too. This was our way of encouraging parents to be actively involved in their children's lives and education. In exchange for meeting the requirements, students receive the equivalent of a full, four-year college scholarship to the public university of their choice within the state. The money can also be applied toward in-state private school tuition.

The first group of Twenty-first Century Scholars entered college in 1995, and today there are thousands more of them in

Indiana colleges or in the pipeline. I remember parents sending me report cards with letters pointing out how well their kids were doing in certain subjects and promising to help them bring up their grades in others. To this day, people still stop me on the street to thank me for that program, telling me what a difference it has made in their lives and in the lives of their children. It's hard for me to describe how heartwarming it is to hear those stories.

4

Responsible Fathers

When you talk about fatherlessness, you're talking about family life, one of the most personal and intimate realms in the human experience.

DURING MY TIME as governor, we also put forth a great deal of effort to curb teen pregnancy. Girls without fathers are more likely to have children as teens, and studies have identified teen pregnancy as one of the best predictors of poverty, under-education, juvenile crime, and welfare dependency. It's a terrible cycle. If a fourteen- or fifteen-year-old girl has a child, there's a strong chance both she and the child will live in poverty—*and* there's a strong chance that the child will grow up to be a teen parent one day, too. To make matters worse, fathers of children born to teen mothers tend to be among the most irresponsible. The girls, of course, bear most of the consequences, because they're the ones who bear the children. And the boys or older men? Often, they just disappear. For too many, the birth is the end of their involvement, not the beginning. Some even consider their irresponsibility a sign of manhood: "I fathered a child. I'm a man." Of course, that's not really what being a mature man is all about. Bringing a child into the world is easy; it's how you treat your child that counts.

I didn't want to create a new state bureaucracy to fight teen pregnancy, but I did want to tackle the issue by helping preexisting efforts at the local level. We brought attention to the problem by holding news conferences with youth groups promoting abstinence, and we started a grant program to bolster local efforts throughout the state, such as the St. Elizabeth's Regional Maternity Center in New Albany. St. Elizabeth's offers pregnancy testing, residential care, medical care, support groups, parenting-skills classes, education assistance, job placement, and counseling. It's a place where a young woman can go to give birth to her child and focus on staying in school and getting health care for herself and the baby. The center has a great success rate, too: 99 percent of the girls don't get pregnant again as teens and the vast majority stay in school. Such programs foster a much better life for both the mother and the child.

Indiana was clearly making progress on issues such as education, teen pregnancy, and welfare. Our state's welfare reforms led the nation in moving people off the welfare rolls and into jobs, and we'd ended eligibility requirements that discouraged unwed parents from getting married. Project RESPECT, our teen pregnancy prevention initiative, was airing TV and radio ads promoting abstinence, and in May of 1996, we distributed nearly one million dollars statewide to local churches, schools, and community organizations to support abstinence education and counseling.

Despite all of this good work, I knew we still weren't getting at the source of these social ills. As politicians, we try to strengthen education by providing more funding for the classroom; we try to make the welfare system more effective and fair by strengthening work requirements; we try to help teen mothers get health care and education. Those efforts are all important, but at some point we need to step back and ask ourselves how to effect prevention, how to stop problems before they happen.

From a policy standpoint, the connection is crystal clear: If you care about raising educational and economic performance, ending welfare dependency, fighting drug and substance abuse, curbing teen pregnancy, and ending juvenile violence, you have to look at how we raise our children. If we fail to nurture and support them and prepare them to deal with life, not only do the children suffer, but society as a whole pays a price.

During my time as governor, social-science research was expanding to include more studies that looked in particular at the effect of father absence. The trend lines were disturbing. Between 1990 and 1996, the number of children living without any adult male in the household had grown from 8 percent to 25 percent. About 40 percent of the children in the United States lived in homes without a father present—more than double the rate in 1960. About 40 percent of those children had not seen their fathers in at least a year; of the remaining 60 percent, only one in six saw his or her father at least once a week.

Indiana was among the states hit hardest by this epidemic. More than 29 percent of families in Indiana did not have a father present in the home—fifth highest in the country. (Indiana subsequently improved somewhat to number seven.) More than 30 percent of the babies born in Indiana were born out of wedlock— ninth highest in the country. More than 74 percent of teen births in Indiana occurred out of wedlock. And the costs to Indiana citizens were continuing to rise as more fathers left mothers to fend for themselves: $50 million for a new juvenile detention center, $64 million a year to deal with the consequences of teenage pregnancy, and $700 million a year to pay welfare to mothers owed child support—to name only a few costs associated with father absence.

What we were facing was a whole culture of fatherlessness, children growing up literally not knowing what it's like to have a dad around—a man who holds down a job, earns a paycheck, and treats Mom with respect and dignity. In many cases, the fathers showed up rarely or not at all, and many of them were abusive toward the mothers of their children. As a result, their kids were growing up without a positive image of male behavior. The boys didn't know how to be men, and the girls didn't know what they should rightfully expect from a man. I remember my policy director, Tom Sugar, telling me about his visit to a sixth-grade elementary-school class. Tom asked the kids, "What is a good father?"

One boy's hand shot up. "A good father is a man who comes around once in a while," he said. "Maybe sometimes he brings diapers for the baby."

As if the boy's answer wasn't chilling enough, it was met with widespread agreement by the other students in the classroom.

Prior to launching a focused attack on fatherlessness, the closest I'd come to tackling the problem head-on was to go after deadbeat dads. Child-support collections were at a historic high thanks in part to efforts such as our "Wanted" posters, which featured the deadbeat Hoosier parents furthest behind in their child-support payments.

I remember the case of one deadbeat dad in particular. During 1991, we'd started a program called Capitol for a Day, where we moved the governor's office from city to city and held open office hours so that citizens could come in off the street and tell us what was on their minds. On the day we were in Marion, a grandmother walked in with her daughter, who was in her early twenties. The daughter was reluctant to talk, so finally the grandmother spoke up and told us that her daughter and grandchild were living in a filthy, rat-infested apartment because the daughter's ex-husband refused to pay child support and had run off to Florida, where he was living in a nice house and owned a speedboat. (The daughter had opted not to go on welfare because she felt it was wrong to take money from the government to support her family when her ex-husband should have been doing it.)

My good friend and director of policy and planning, Richard Gordon, contacted the governor's office in Florida, but they couldn't help—in those days, the laws didn't provide for reciprocity in such cases. We thought we were at a dead end until the grandmother called one day to tell us that her ex-son-in-law was coming back to town for the Indianapolis 500 time trials. We got the state police on the case right away and had the man arrested as soon as he arrived in Indianapolis, at which time he became a guest of the state.

When they hauled the man into court, the judged asked him, "Will you pay?"

"No," the man said, and so back to jail he went. The judge wouldn't release him, because once he left the state, we'd lose jurisdiction. Again and again he was brought before the judge, and each time he refused to pay. Finally, after six months in custody, the man gave in.

That was the last we heard of the case until the following January, when Richard received a note in the mail from the man's seven-year-old daughter. She said that thanks to our help, she and her mother had been able to move into a better home, and she'd just enjoyed her first real Christmas.

When it comes to unpaid child support, however, you can't rely on only one approach, because you're basically dealing with two different groups of fathers (and the occasional mother). You have the dads who *can* pay and choose not to, usually because of disagreements with the mother, and the belief that their money isn't actually going to their kids. These are the deadbeat dads. Then you have another class of individuals who *can't* pay—the dead-broke dads, men without jobs or money. Collecting child support from them is like trying to get blood from a stone. Ideally, the government would help dead-broke dads get back on their feet so they can support their kids, but most are high-school dropouts, lacking the skills for decent jobs, and many have substance-abuse problems. This is a difficult group to help, but in order to improve the lives of children, we must enable those parents to do their part.

The cycle of illiteracy offers a useful analogy. Susan founded the Indiana Literacy Foundation and made illiteracy her principal issue as First Lady of Indiana. As she can tell you, the problem tends to run in families because parents who can't read don't teach their kids to read, and they typically don't have books and newspapers and magazines around the house to pique their kids' interest in reading. By getting a parent to read, you give a child a better chance of becoming a reader. It's all about breaking cycles, whether it be the cycle of illiteracy or the cycle of poverty that breeds dead-broke dads.

In my second term as governor, I began looking for ways to more directly address the problem of father absence. I knew that government alone couldn't solve the problem, but I felt that the state government must support the values of our communities and take action to help.

During my State of the State address in January 1996, two months after my sons were born, I stood before the Indiana General

Assembly and held up a birth certificate on which the space provided for the father's name had been left blank. I wanted Indiana's citizens and lawmakers to think about how difficult life must be for a child who never knows his or her father. I also wanted to drive home the point that we were seeing too many of these birth certificates in Indiana and across the country.

A high-profile gathering of experts in the field—public and private, religious and secular, practitioners and academics—seemed like a good next step. One of the difficulties of building public support for fatherhood initiatives is that father absence is a complicated, little-understood topic. People still need to be educated about it. If you tell a gathering of citizens, "We've got to do something about these delinquents who are committing violent crimes and preying upon innocent people," or, "Let's ensure that our kids don't get involved with drugs and alcohol," everybody in the crowd will say "Absolutely." But as soon as you tell that same crowd that we need to hold fathers responsible for the children they bring into the world, a lot of those people will shrug their shoulders and look blank. They don't recognize the connection between fatherlessness and other social problems.

One of the difficulties in building *political* support for fatherhood initiatives is that father absence is an incredibly sensitive topic. When you talk about fatherlessness, you're talking about family life, one of the most personal and intimate realms in the human experience. There's reluctance on the part of many public figures to get involved with debates on sex, marriage, or child-rearing, because they don't want to say anything that might offend. But if our country is going to make real progress against our most pressing social challenges, such as juvenile crime and drug and alcohol addiction, we can no longer afford to be in denial about the consequences of fatherlessness.

My hope was that a large-scale conference on fatherhood would raise public awareness about the issue and build political support as well. I also hoped it would provide a hands-on forum where experts and practitioners could compare notes, bolstering the various fatherhood programs that already existed in the state. When you're dealing with problems like strengthening families and saving children, you don't just pass a law—that's the easy part. If the conference was going to really make a difference, we had to bring together people who were on the front lines in the fight for responsible fatherhood and empower them to do something about it.

In May of 1996, we put out a call to the whole state: If you care about fatherhood issues, if you're working to address fatherhood issues, if you've *thought* about working to address them, come to Indianapolis for the Governor's Conference on Fatherhood. On September 24, close to a thousand people showed up at the Indiana Convention Center, including representatives of more than forty different initiatives from fifteen states—the largest such gathering of its kind in the nation up to that time. The theme of the conference was "Restoring Fatherhood, Renewing Families." Throughout the day, experts participated in presentations designed to help Hoosiers learn about the diverse approaches being used across the country to improve the relationship between fathers and their families. The programs were designed to reach fathers from all walks of life, and they included efforts based in schools, religious institutions, community centers, health-care facilities, prisons, and neighborhoods. It was my hope that Hoosiers, armed with knowledge gained at the conference, would go out and apply that knowledge across the state, raising the standard of fatherhood in Indiana to such a level that we might one day serve as a model for the country. The cause of responsible fatherhood had truly become my own, and it would work its way into and then become a key issue in my public policy efforts from that day forward.

The conference also gave me an opportunity to meet a number of people in the growing fatherhood movement, including Dr. Wade Horn, who was director of the National Fatherhood Initiative and today is the Assistant Secretary for Children and Families in the Department of Health and Human Services. Founded in 1994, the NFI has done more than any other organization to help our society confront the problem of father absence. Our conference helped the NFI establish a foothold in Indiana. Five years later, thanks in part to ties forged on that September day and work I did with my colleagues in the Senate, our state became only the fourth in the country with its own NFI program.

However, the conference was only the first step in our effort to promote responsible fatherhood in Indiana. We also launched a statewide ad campaign to raise awareness of the issue, using a series of ads produced by the National Fatherhood Initiative. With the ad campaign, we were trying to change society's attitudes about parenthood, particularly among young people who might consider bringing a child into the world regardless of whether they're married or can support the child. The reasons for teen pregnancy are sometimes more complex than simply a careless act without thought for consequences. Young women—especially those who don't grow up in the best circumstances and suffer from personal insecurities— sometimes choose to have a child because they want someone who will love them unconditionally, who will perhaps give them the kind of affection they didn't get from their own parents. Young men all too often have no real sense of the commitment or responsibility that fatherhood involves.

I found one of the ads to be particularly powerful. It opened with an all-American image of a young boy wearing a ball cap and a baseball mitt, playing catch. You see the boy throwing the ball; you see him picking it up from the grass. Then the camera pulls back and you realize the boy is all alone, playing catch with himself. The parent you expect to see isn't there. When Senator Joe Lieberman saw the ad a few years later at the press conference where I introduced The Responsible Fatherhood Act, he said it almost brought tears to his eyes.

We wanted to get as much exposure as possible for the ads, so I arranged to meet with general managers of several television stations. "Look," I said, "this is the first time in history we're going to put money on the table to buy television ads. Now we expect you to step up to the plate and join us." I asked them to sell us spots at two for the price of one, three for one. And they came through.

Public education about father absence is important, but it isn't enough. You have to back it up with programs that impact real people. Furthermore, no single program model is adequate. A variety of programs are needed to address a variety of family circumstances and a variety of dads—divorced and separated dads, stepfathers, incarcerated dads, unwed dads, teen dads, adoptive fathers, foster fathers. Also, it's important to remember that there are many *married* dads out there who still need the knowledge and skills to be competent fathers. Finally, programs must not only help fathers connect with their kids; they must also reach out to those children who have no fathers. These boys and girls need to be mentored so that when they become men and women, they'll understand what a good father is even if they haven't been fortunate enough to have one of their own.

So, in addition to the conference and the TV ads, we started a grant program to provide direct support to the many programs across the state that were promoting responsible fatherhood and related causes. The conference helped people learn how to tackle the problem; the grant program provided capital for them to put their knowledge to use. The fatherhood movement had begun as a grassroots effort, and by 1996, many programs had already been established across the state. Some were church-based, some were community-based. It didn't matter. Our rule was, if a program had a track record of success, Indiana's government wanted to provide that program with grant money so it could expand its activities.

To date, the Indiana fatherhood grants have helped more than nineteen thousand Hoosiers through a variety of programs. One such program is the Security Dads at Arlington High School on Indianapolis' east side, a group of fathers who patrol the hallways and let the students know that there are adult men who care about the school. It's an important kind of program: A Department of Education study indicates that a child is more likely to do well in school if his or her father is involved with the school, attending its activities and events. The program has an especially strong impact on those young men who have no positive male role model at home. I'd visited Arlington High School and been so impressed that I declared May 8, 1995, to be Security Dads Day in Indiana. Seeing such programs in action has always brought me great satisfaction. It's one thing to think about an issue academically or conceptually; it's another to actually see it being put into practice.

Our grant program was able to help children by providing much-needed financial support to such outstanding programs. And ultimately, that's what the fatherhood movement is all about: trying to give every child in America the best chance of growing up to have a successful life. Whenever I need to remember that, all I have to do is think back to a visit I made to the Tolson Park Youth Center in Elkhart, Indiana. The youth center was located in a rundown, drug-infested area, but we'd provided a grant that allowed the neighborhood to clean up the building and turn it into a learning and recreation center. They had desks and books in the front of the building and a basketball court, foosball, billiards, and a snack bar in the back. After the kids did an hour's worth of academic work, they were allowed to go in the back and play.

The press was there on the day I visited, and several cameramen were following me around the rec center when I came across two little girls in pigtails. They were maybe ten or eleven years old. They were kind of nervous as I chatted with them about their schoolwork. They looked over at the cameras, and they looked at me, and then one of them said, "Sir, why do those people think you're so important?"

Leave it to an eleven-year-old to stump the governor. I had to think about her question for a minute.

"Well, sweetheart," I told her. "They think I'm important because I'm the governor of the state, but the truth of the matter is, you're the one who's important, because you're the reason I'm here."

That answer seemed to make sense to her, and it still makes good sense to me.

When these youngsters and I planted this tree, we agreed that if it was well cared for, it would grow tall and strong. The same applies to children, and there's a saying I'm very fond of: "Children are the living messages we send to a time we will not see."

In March of 1996 I signed my last bill into law as governor of Indiana, putting the finishing touches on an ambitious education reform program that established high academic standards and increased accountability for our schools. To mark the occasion, I visited with these young students at Central Elementary School in Pike Township in Indianapolis.

Since my earliest days as governor, I've wanted to give Indiana's children the best possible chance of reaching their full potential. Visiting classrooms and being able to spend time with children were among the high points of my terms.

Under Zachary's Law, the State of Indiana maintains a registry of individuals convicted of sex offenses against minors. Sandy Snider—the mother of Zachary Snider, for whom the law was named—and her daughter Caitlin joined me to celebrate the signing of the law in March 1994.

5

MY PARENTS

*Both of my parents were very accomplished public
speakers, which is how they met.*

IN DEALING WITH legislation and programs that promote
responsible fatherhood, I've frequently had occasion to think hard
about my own life—not only as a father, but also as a son. Research
tells us that family plays a crucial role in shaping who we are, and
certainly my parents have influenced every aspect of my life, from
my values and priorities, to my choice of a career in politics, to the
way I've raised my own sons.

My family is from Terre Haute, Indiana. My father, Birch Evans
Bayh, Jr., was born there on January 22, 1928. Birch Bayh, Sr., my
grandfather, was born in the small town of Patricksburg and
graduated from nearby Clay Central High School, where he met his
future wife, Leah Hollingsworth. My grandfather served as an army
lieutenant during World War I and then settled in Terre Haute,
where he joined the faculty at Indiana Normal (now Indiana State
University) and became the school's first athletic director, thus
beginning his lifelong devotion to physical fitness and sports. He
was for many years a famous referee, officiating more championship

games of the boys' high-school basketball tournament than anyone else—a great honor in a state such as Indiana, where basketball comes close to being the official state religion. The Indiana Basketball Hall of Fame in New Castle features an exhibit on officiating that includes a jersey and program from a game my grandfather refereed, and from time to time, I still run into people who remember him.

In 1989, shortly after I was elected governor, I had the pleasure of meeting John Wooden, who'd played his high-school ball at Martinsville before going on to become a Purdue All-American and a longtime coach at UCLA—perhaps the greatest college basketball coach ever. He was in Martinsville for the dedication ceremony of a new gymnasium. When we were introduced, he smiled fondly. "Ah, your grandfather," Wooden said. "He blew a very fair whistle."

On another occasion, I met Red Auerbach, the famous coach and general manager who led the Boston Celtics to sixteen championships and nine NBA titles, the greatest dynasty in NBA history. "You know, your granddad got me started," he said, chomping on his cigar. He told me that my grandfather had hired him as a coach at Roosevelt High School in Washington, D.C. From there, Auerbach went on to coach two now-defunct pro teams, the Washington Capitols and Tri-Cities Blackhawks, before signing on with the Celtics.

Washington is where my grandfather settled after leaving Terre Haute, taking a job as director of physical education for the District's public schools. My father spent much of his adolescence in the nation's capital. When he was twelve, his mother, Leah, died of uterine cancer, so when my grandfather went off to World War II the following year to serve as an Air Force colonel in charge of physical fitness for U.S. troops in the China-Burma theater, my father and his sister, Mary Alice, moved back to Indiana to live with their maternal grandparents—Mr. and Mrs. John Harrison Hollingsworth—on their farm in Shirkieville.

As a teenager growing up on the farm, my father took a real liking to agriculture. He enjoyed working with the livestock, planting things, watching them grow. After high school, he enrolled at Purdue, supplementing his first-year tuition with earnings from his summer job as a field hand picking tomatoes for the Campbell soup plant near our farm. To this day, he loves fresh red tomatoes, as do I. He says they used to pick those tomatoes and eat them like apples right there in the field.

That love of farming was still with my father years later when he was in the Senate and we were living in Washington, D.C., on Garfield Street in a neighborhood called Cleveland Park. During the summer of 1979, after my mother passed away, he actually plowed up the side yard and planted a big garden—corn, tomatoes, green beans, and so forth. The neighbors' reactions were mixed. Some of them were aghast at the idea of farming in a city neighborhood; others liked the garden and would stop by to see how it was coming along. I used to tell people that my father got the best yield per acre of anybody in northwest Washington. In fact, he still plants tomatoes and cucumbers at his home in Chevy Chase, Maryland, and Nick and Beau help pick them at harvest time. It's great to see our agricultural heritage handed down, at least in part.

My father left Purdue at the end of his freshman year for a two-year stint in the army. It was during his time in the service that my father began to make a name for himself. That's where he learned to box, and he later went on to win a Golden Gloves championship. He also began to take an interest in public service. He was stationed in Germany, a country struggling to recover from the war. The

Germans were very poor at the time, and food was in short supply. Using seeds that he'd brought from Indiana, my father spent his spare time teaching German children how to plant gardens and raise food for themselves—a one-soldier predecessor of the Peace Corps, as my mother once said. A story about him entitled "The G.I. Ambassador" appeared in *Reader's Digest*. After he got out of the army, he came back to Purdue, where he played varsity baseball, was selected for his fraternity's highest national honor, and was elected class president. Then, in 1951, he met my mother.

My mother, Marvella Hern, was born on February 14, 1933, in Enid, Oklahoma, and grew up in the Dust Bowl. My father's parents weren't well-to-do by any stretch of the imagination, but my mother's parents were of even more modest means. Her father, Delbert Hern, was a wheat farmer, and her mother, Bernett, worked as a telephone operator at nearby Vance Air Force Base. Later in life, Delbert experienced some financial setbacks, became an alcoholic, and took his own life and the life of his second wife. It was a very tragic situation and especially heartbreaking to my mother, who idolized her father. (My mother, by the way, was *not* the daughter of former Indiana governor Matt Welsh, as has been reported occasionally in the press.)

I've heard people describe my mother as having a sparkling personality. She was vivacious, popular, and outgoing—not unlike Susan in many ways. (She often used to tell me, "I hope you'll marry a girl who will bring out the best in you," and I did.) Her good cheer was all the more impressive considering the various health problems she endured throughout her life. As a child, she contracted measles, which affected her vision. She also had a weight problem when she was very young—the result of a thyroid imbalance—and she had to count calories the rest of her life. (Fortunately, she had an iron will.)

In 1954, she and my father were in a terrible auto accident that left her in a coma for more than two weeks and broke her clavicle and her foot. As a result of the wreck, she suffered double vision off and on for the rest of her life. Ten years later, they were in a plane crash that broke her tailbone. Then, in 1971, she was diagnosed with breast cancer. She'd had a very early menopause, and in those days, they treated early menopause with large doses of estrogen. Doctors now believe there may be a link between estrogen and breast cancer, but whether that was the reason she contracted cancer, we'll never know.

Despite her health problems, my mother was a very successful woman. At Enid High School, she was Band Queen and the first female student body president. In 1950, she was elected governor of Girls State in Oklahoma and then president of Girls Nation, earning herself a trip to the White House and a meeting with President Truman. (When she was running for governor of Girls State, one of her campaign posters hung in bathroom stalls: DON'T JUST SIT THERE. VOTE FOR MARVELLA!)

In 1967, President Lyndon Johnson asked her to be the vice-chairman of the Democratic National Committee—a significant invitation for a woman in that time of male-dominated politics. She wanted the job desperately, but she and my father decided that she would turn down the president's offer so that she could help with my father's Senate reelection campaign. The decision grated on her for a long time, and, if he had it to do over again, I believe my father would insist that she take the position.

She was a very talented woman who'd never really pursued a career because, in those days, women just didn't do such things. But after my father won the election, my mother was determined to explore some of her own interests. Following her diagnosis with breast cancer, she became the chief public spokesperson for the American Cancer Society. She was one of the first women to go public with her condition, and she was very involved with Reach to Recovery, a program that offered support to women with breast cancer. She even had a brief television career in 1976, hosting a weekly segment about the Bicentennial for a local NBC affiliate in Washington.

Both of my parents were very accomplished public speakers, which is how they met. Birch and Marvella were attending a national Farm Bureau speaking contest in Chicago on December 10, 1951. My father was representing Indiana, and my mother, who was in her freshman year at Oklahoma A&M (now Oklahoma State), was representing Oklahoma. There's a wonderful picture from the morning of the contest: In a reception room full of contestants, my father sits at a table with other members of the Indiana delegation; at the edge of the picture, a woman's foot is visible. That's my mother's foot, and a moment after the picture was taken, my father turned around and introduced himself.

My father had already won two state Farm Bureau contests, and my mother figured he'd win this national contest as well. As it turns out, *she* won—the first girl ever to do so—beating three boys in the final round, which was held in the Grand Ballroom of the Stevens Hotel in front of thousands of farmers attending the American Farm Bureau convention. (My father had been knocked out in an earlier round.) On the final night of the convention, they went on their first date, dining at the Ivanhoe Club and driving all over Chicago in my father's blue 1950 Studebaker.

After that night, she returned to college in Oklahoma, and my father returned to the farm in Shirkieville, where he and Granddaddy Hollingsworth lived. My father visited Enid in January, my mother visited Indiana that April, and then she enrolled in summer school at Indiana State Teachers' College in Terre Haute, the same school where my grandfather had once served on the faculty.

Later that summer, Birch Bayh and Marvella Hern were married in Enid's Methodist church on August 24, 1952, a muggy Sunday afternoon. She was only nineteen; he was twenty-four. They settled on the farm in Shirkieville, which sits near Highway 150, west of Terre Haute. It's just a couple miles short of the Illinois border, about as far west as you can go and still be in Indiana. My mother continued her studies at Indiana State, and my father ran the farm. He grew corn and soybeans and even tried his hand at raising hogs.

In 1954, at the age of twenty-six, my father decided to run as a Democrat for the Indiana state legislature. He was up against a candidate who had the backing of the political machine in Vigo County, which was very powerful in those days, but my father campaigned energetically, going out and meeting lots of voters. He scored an upset victory and was sworn in on January 7, 1955. After he served his first session, he and my mother decided to have a baby, a fortunate decision since it turned out she was already pregnant. I was born later that year, in Terre Haute's Union Hospital, on the day after Christmas.

My father's job required a fair amount of travel around the state, and he and my mother took me along whenever they could. Supporters at political functions would often pitch in to help look after me, and these days, kindly older women still come up and tell me that they once babysat me or changed my diaper. Judging from the number of times I've heard this, I can only assume I was the driest baby in Indiana.

Following his reelection to the state legislature, my father had a tough decision to make. He loved farming, but he loved his work as a legislator, too, and it was becoming increasingly hard to do both. Also, he was barely making ends meet on the farm. He briefly took an office job in Terre Haute with the Hulman Company, working for Tony Hulman, who owned the Indianapolis Speedway, and then he left that job to serve his second term in the 1957 legislature.

At the end of the 1957 session, my dad decided to put all his energy into politics. He left the farm and enrolled in law school at Indiana University. It was a big gamble for a young father. To cover tuition, he had to sell the farmhouse and part of the land. We moved to Bloomington in October 1957, and while my dad attended law school, my mother resumed her undergraduate coursework. Our little family lived in married-student housing, a two-bedroom apartment on Hoosier Courts. It was so cramped that my father had to store important state documents under the bed. I attended IU Nursery School co-op, a kindergarten for the children of married students. I remember carving my first jack-o'-lantern in Bloomington, and I remember the ice cream truck, its bell ringing at the same time every afternoon. Even though money was tight in those days, my mother later said she was never happier.

The two years following Dwight Eisenhower's reelection in 1956 were a sorry time for Democrats in Indiana. The Republican Party dominated the state. So few Democrats had been elected to the House that they couldn't even break a quorum. As a result of the Democrats' powerlessness, few of them had much interest in serving in leadership positions. My father was an exception. He ran for and won the post of minority leader in 1957. Two years later, the political tide turned. A recession hit the nation, and a scandal in the state highway department tarnished the image of the Republican governor. Lo and behold, in the 1958 election, the Democrats won in a landslide. They went from being powerless to being the majority party, and my father went from being minority leader to Speaker of the House in 1959. He was thirty years old, the youngest Speaker ever. There's a great picture of him that still hangs in the General Assembly of the statehouse, a very young man sitting with the other party leaders in a conservative suit and tie, black wing-tipped shoes—and white socks.

He was Speaker of the House for two years. The Republicans then regained control and he went back to being the minority leader in 1961. It was from that position, energized by the election of John F. Kennedy, that he would launch his bid for the United States Senate.

6
MY FATHER, THE SENATOR

*Dinners at the White House may sound
glamorous, and they were, but such events were
the exception for me, not the rule.*

MY PARENTS HAD graduated together from Indiana University on June 6, 1960, and moved back to Terre Haute, where my father practiced law and continued to serve as a state legislator. We lived on Jackson Street in a neighborhood called Edgewood Grove, with sunflowers growing in our backyard next to the garage. I was a few weeks too young to begin first grade that fall, so rather than have me hanging around the house that year, lying fallow, my mother got me involved in a variety of lessons, including swimming at the YMCA, music, and—of all things—tap dancing, which she thought would be good for my dexterity (I've never put on a pair of tap shoes since). The following year, I started first grade at Meadows Elementary, which was only two or three blocks from our house. Fortuitously, there was a Dairy Queen not far beyond the school. I remember getting my first bike in Terre Haute, sledding at Deming Park, learning to hit a baseball, flying kites next to the school, and going to church at Centenary Methodist Church, where both of my parents taught Sunday school classes. I can't help looking back on those times as the Norman Rockwell years of my life. I had a loving family. We lived in a close-knit community. Crime was something that happened to other people in other places. Neighbors watched after each other's children. I suppose I remember my childhood in Terre Haute the same way the country tends to remember the 1950s and early 1960s in general—things didn't seem quite so complicated then.

In 1961, my father began campaigning for the U.S. Senate, formally announcing his candidacy in Indianapolis at the Claypool Hotel on October 19. He and my mother had decided that he would give it his best shot, putting all his resources and energy into this one campaign. If it didn't work out, he'd leave politics and devote himself to the practice of law. He and my mother both campaigned, traveling separately in order to cover more of the state. At Christmas, they took a break so we could visit my mother's family in Oklahoma, and on the way back, we stopped to see Harry Truman at his home in Independence, Missouri.

My mother had first met Truman when she was president of Girls Nation, and when my father decided to run for the Senate, Delbert Hern, my mother's father, wrote to Truman and asked if he'd meet with my father to give him advice. (My grandfather had an interest in public issues at the time, having run unsuccessfully for sheriff and for the Oklahoma state legislature and having served as a county Democratic chairman. I remember riding around in the back of his pickup as he distributed his campaign material.) Truman wrote back and said he'd be happy to meet with my father, so we all piled into the car and headed to Missouri—my parents, my grandparents, and me, dressed in my one little dark-blue suit and tie.

My mother was a loving person, but she was also strict when it involved children's manners. During the drive, she admonished me to behave at Truman's. "Children are to be seen and not heard," she said. "We're bringing you on an important trip. You just sit there and listen and pay attention."

When we arrived at Truman's big frame house, he invited us in and gave me a silver dollar—a memorable gift, as I'm told he was quite frugal. My mother had made me promise to be on my best behavior, and I was, but after a half hour, the cans of soda pop I'd drunk on the long car ride worked their way through my system and would not be denied. Just about the time my father and Truman started talking political strategy, I blurted out, "Mom, I've got to go to the bathroom!" She was mortified, but Truman saved the day. He stood up and said, "That's all right, young man. So do I." He grabbed my hand and off we went.

My father's opponent in the Senate race was Republican Homer Capehart, an eighteen-year incumbent. Nobody gave my father a chance; in fact, few people even thought he'd get the Democratic nomination. In those days, the Senate nominees were decided at a state convention, rather than through the primaries that are used today. My father was up against Charles Boswell, the sitting mayor of Indianapolis; Jack Edwards, the mayor of Marion; and Judge John Gonas of South Bend. My earliest political memory is from that convention, sitting in the stands at the State Fairgrounds Coliseum in June 1962. It was a good old-fashioned convention, with hats, balloons, bands, posters—even two donkeys, Jack and Jackie, named for the Kennedys. I was too young to really know what was going on, but I knew it was big, and I knew it involved my parents. Each of them had a walkie-talkie and was followed across the convention floor by a campaign worker carrying a twenty-foot pole with their picture at the top, which is how they kept track of each other as they worked the noisy crowd. In the end, my father was able to win the nomination thanks to his tireless campaigning and the backing of the governor, Matt Welsh. Supporting Birch Bayh was a risky political move for the governor, though. Some of his top advisors wanted him to endorse the mayor of Indianapolis, because there were quite a few Democratic legislators from the Indianapolis area, and the governor needed their support for his legislative program.

Getting the nomination was tough, but it was still viewed as a Pyrrhic victory, since Capehart was expected to trounce my father in the general election. Nevertheless, my father won—by less than two votes per precinct, only ten thousand votes statewide. It was a huge upset. Capehart had perhaps gotten a little complacent, whereas my father had campaigned as hard as he possibly could, driving all over the state, sleeping in his car, visiting innumerable coffee shops, factory gates, anywhere he could meet with voters. He had some good help—starting with my mother, who also campaigned at a breakneck pace. Truman came to Indiana to speak on his behalf, as did President Kennedy on October 13. Even though Kennedy had lost Indiana by more than 200,000 votes in 1960, his election had spurred a youth movement in politics. The country was emerging from the 1950s, and voters were looking for more energetic leaders.

My father was reelected six years later after running against Bill Ruckelshaus, a very formidable state senator who went on to become the first head of the U.S. Environmental Protection Agency. He won again in 1974 against former Rhodes Scholar Dick Lugar, who was then the mayor of Indianapolis and is now my colleague and a five-term senator, the longest-serving senator in Indiana history (my father is tied for second place with three terms).

I was in the middle of second grade when my father was first elected to the Senate. We moved to the Chesterbrook Woods development in McLean, Virginia, in the middle of December 1962. On the morning we left, a blizzard had so frozen Terre Haute that the newspaper photographers who'd gathered to see us off had to thaw their cameras in our oven.

The move was traumatic for me as a seven-year-old—being uprooted from my school, having to say good-bye to all my friends—but our next-door neighbors, the Waltons, did a very kind thing that helped to soften the blow. They said that if my father won the election, their big collie, Duffy, could come to Washington with us. Duffy had taken a liking to me and slept under my bedroom window at night, and having him next to me there on the backseat made the long car ride to Washington much more bearable.

Two months later, on the night before Valentine's Day, my parents were invited to dinner at the White House—the first of many such occasions. Vice President Johnson took a quick liking to them, my mother in particular, since he and she were from the same part of the country.

One night in 1965, a couple of years after LBJ assumed the presidency following Kennedy's assassination, the president called with a last-minute dinner invitation. My parents had already eaten, but that didn't matter: when the president invites you to the White House, you go. The only problem was, they couldn't find a sitter for me on such short notice. When my mother called back to say they couldn't come, the president would hear none of it.

"Bring the boy along," he said.

An hour later, we joined seven or eight other guests at the dinner table in the private quarters of the White House. My mother wanted me to make a good impression. Before dinner, she'd told me, "If you're confused about which knife and fork to use, just look to the person next to you and see what they're doing." I was getting along just fine until the waiter brought out a bowl of water with a lemon slice floating in it. I'd never seen such a thing before, and I had no idea what to do. Eat it like soup? Dip the bread in it? Mrs. Johnson must have seen the bewildered look on my face.

"That's called a finger bowl," she said. "I didn't know what it was either at first." Then she showed me what to do. Later, she could tell I was getting bored with the adults' talk, so she took my hand and led me into another room. Soon I was sitting on Abe Lincoln's bed watching television. What caught my attention was the remote control. In those days, *nobody* had a remote control to change channels. It seemed to me like something out of a James Bond movie, a super-secret device that only the CIA could dream up.

I'll never forget the way LBJ leaned back in his chair and proceeded to put both his feet up on the table that night. "That's pretty cool," I thought, "the president of the United States, putting his feet up on the dinner table." When we got home, however, my mother let me know in a hurry that such behavior might be okay for presidents, but it wasn't okay for nine-year-old boys.

Dinners at the White House may sound glamorous, and they were, but such events were the exception for me, not the rule. And as a kid, I don't really think those visits made a very strong impression on me (except for that remote control). At the time, I was more concerned with going to school, winning Little League games, and playing with Duffy—the kind of things that are important to any nine-year-old.

The classes at Chesterbrook Elementary in McLean were larger than those back in Terre Haute, and my parents worried I wasn't being sufficiently challenged. I think the final straw was the "crook book" I brought home from school one day, a notebook my friends and I had filled with drawings of various criminals in prison garb and stories about the exotic crimes they'd committed. We'd been working on it during class because the teacher was busy with students who needed extra help. My parents let me finish second grade at Chesterbrook, but the next fall, they sent me to Fairfax Christian Day School, a new fundamentalist Christian school. The following year, they decided I would attend the more established, nonreligious Potomac School, where I completed fourth and fifth grade.

Then, in August of 1967, we moved from the suburbs of Virginia into the District of Columbia. Our house was about seven blocks from St. Albans, an Episcopalian boys' school affiliated with the National Cathedral. That's where I went from sixth grade until the end of high school. Religious faith was important to my mother in those days and would become even more so in later years, and she and my father both liked the fact that St. Albans was religiously affiliated. Looking back on it, I'm grateful as well that I received some religious instruction. At St. Albans, we attended chapel a couple of times a week, plus occasional services at the National Cathedral. Nick and Beau's school, Beauvoir, is also affiliated with the National Cathedral.

During the summers, I'd usually go back to our family farm in Shirkieville for a week or two, then visit my second cousins in Martinsville, where we'd fish and ride horses. Beginning in 1967, I spent four summers at Culver Military Academy in Culver, Indiana, on Lake Maxinkuckee, near Plymouth. I didn't mind wearing the uniform or marching in formation, and I loved the canoeing and sailing, the horseback riding, the swimming and sports. My mother liked Culver because I learned to fold my clothes and make my bed. Those last two summers, my best friend Steven Sinnenberg (son of my mother's close friend Jane) attended Culver as well. In the summer of 1969, I caught the flu while I was there, and I remember lying in my bunk watching a black-and-white TV when Neil Armstrong became the first man to set foot on the moon.

As an only child, I came to value the camaraderie and companionship I found at Culver. That's one reason I've always liked team sports—especially soccer, basketball, football, and baseball. I'm glad that my sons have each other for company, but it's not as if I spent my own youth wishing for a sibling. I always had best friends who were like brothers to me. And in a way, it's probably good that I was an only child. My father was gone a great deal, and both of my parents stayed very busy. If I'd had brothers or sisters, my parents would have been hard-pressed to give us the attention that they would have wanted to give us, and finances—occasionally an issue around our dinner table—would have been tighter.

7

GROWING UP IN THE PUBLIC EYE

*I was his son, and I loved him like a son—our
relationship was never based on his status as a
political figure—but anytime you work on a
campaign, you also develop a strong belief in what
you're doing and who you're trying to help.*

IN THE FALL of 1971, when I was fifteen years old, my mother was
diagnosed with breast cancer. She was thirty-nine years old. She
entered the Columbia Hospital for Women on October 8 for a
modified radical mastectomy in which the doctors removed her
right breast, lymph glands, and some chest muscle. At the time, my
father was seeking the 1972 Democratic nomination for president,
and his campaign was just starting to pick up steam. Five days after
my mother's surgery, he held a press conference.

"Whenever I have had an important decision to make during
the seventeen years I have had the good fortune to serve in public
life, my wife, Marvella, has always been there," he told the packed
room. "But Marvella is not here today. She is not here because she
underwent critical surgery for a malignancy." He went on to explain
that he wanted to be by her side during her recuperation, and,
therefore, he was not a candidate for president.

My mother's operation was a success, and after several grueling chemotherapy and radiation treatments, she appeared to have beaten cancer. Three years later, in 1974, she began her involvement with the American Cancer Society, volunteering as the cochairman of the organization's 1974 Cancer Crusade. I graduated from high school that spring and went back home to Indiana to work on my father's reelection campaign and start college at Indiana University. After my freshman year, in 1975, I returned to Washington and spent the first of three summers working construction on the Metro, Washington's rail system—first as a laborer, then as a miner, then on a crew laying track.

I'd gotten my first construction job back in high school, working on a housing project when I was sixteen. That summer I think I made three dollars and twenty-five cents an hour. Now, working on the Metro, I had a union job, which paid significantly better—maybe six or six-fifty an hour. Like a lot of guys my age, I was saving up for a car. I ended up buying a used but sporty convertible that I thought would impress the girls. It broke down six blocks away from the dealership.

Both of my parents, my mother in particular, had encouraged me to do physical labor because they'd both grown up on a farm, where you worked hard all day, year round, with no vacation. They thought it was important that I learn the value of hard work, and it *was* hard. We'd already have broken a good sweat by the time commuters drove past on their way to work, and we'd still be out there when they were heading home.

I'd like for my children to have similar jobs at some point. Even if my boys grow up to have office jobs, I think they ought to know how fortunate they are. Physical labor teaches you determination, the value of a dollar, the importance of an education. It teaches you to respect people who do that kind of work for a living, and it guards against any sense of elitism that sometimes arises from being the beneficiary of life's advantages.

One summer, we usually worked from six in the morning until six in the evening, because the project was perpetually behind schedule and the contractors were at risk of getting fined. Ours was a rough-and-tumble crew. The boss let me drive the company dump truck because I was the only one he trusted to bring it back.

The guys at the construction site thought my name was Ed Bays, and I didn't bother to correct them. I didn't really want them to know that I was the son of a senator. Sometimes, though, I was slow to remember my new moniker. They'd shout, "Ed! Hey, Ed! Are you deaf or something?"

These jobs gave me great empathy for the struggle of people limited by a lack of education. We used to have crew meetings each Monday morning during which the foreman and shop steward would gather us to go over the safety report for the week. My first day on the job, the foreman looked up at the group and said, "Okay, who here is a reader?"

After an awkward pause, I said haltingly, "I read a little."

"All right, Bays. Get your butt up here."

So I went up and read the safety report. Then the foreman told everybody to sign the report to certify that they'd heard it. A couple of the guys couldn't write their own names; they just made a mark on the sheet. That was the first time I'd been around people who couldn't read, and I had to stop and remind myself how fortunate I was.

Years later, I ran into the owner of the Atlas Track Company, and he told me I was the only young person who ever wrote him a thank-you note for a summer job, a courtesy my parents had always insisted on. As a kid, it's hard to appreciate what a lasting impression gratitude and good manners make, and I want my sons to learn about that, too. I know I certainly never expected the owner of Atlas Track to remember my note after all that time.

Over the years, I also worked on three of my father's political campaigns. Those campaigns (even the losing presidential bid in 1976 and the failed Senate reelection campaign in 1980) brought us closer together. I was his son, and I loved him like a son—our relationship was never based on his status as a political figure—but anytime you work on a campaign, you also develop a strong belief in what you're doing and who you're trying to help. To say that I idolized him would not be much of an overstatement.

I was too young to work on his first presidential bid, but a couple years later, during the summer after I graduated from high school, I volunteered for his 1974 reelection campaign, making speeches, passing out literature, doing whatever was needed. When my father made another run at the presidency in 1976, I took off the second semester of my sophomore year at IU to volunteer again. That campaign was a transforming experience. I spoke on his behalf in Iowa, New Hampshire, and Massachusetts; I stayed in supporters' homes; I gave press interviews. Even though my father dropped out on March 4 after a disappointing showing in the Massachusetts primary, I had discovered how exhilarating it could be to work for a cause and a candidate in whom you believe. There's a saying about people who've been bitten by the political bug: "The politics doesn't come out until the formaldehyde goes in." I hope it's not true of me, but I understand how it happens.

I wrote a paper about that election for one of my classes at IU. My father had waited until October 21, 1975, to announce his candidacy, barely a year before the election and only three months before the crucial Iowa caucus. I felt that he would have had a better shot if he'd thrown his hat into the ring earlier—and that he would have done so if my mother had supported him earlier. Today, as a forty-seven-year-old, I'd write that paper differently than I did as a twenty-year-old sophomore, because I now understand the poignant difficulties of that decision. My mother had some pretty strong reasons for not wanting him to run for president in 1976, not the least of which was that she'd had cancer and didn't know how long she would live. She'd always been an enthusiastic supporter of my father's career, but since she'd been sick, she'd started to ask herself, "Is this really all we want to do with our lives?" Campaigns were getting more expensive, they were getting nastier, and they required a candidate to be away from home more often. Most of their friends made more money and didn't face the financial pressures my parents did. I think that she was ready to move on. But I was a twenty-year-old college kid—what did I know? My father was running for president of the United States. I didn't think about cancer, campaign finances, or the nuances of politics. I just believed in my father and thought it would be a great thing for the country if he were elected, and there were no two sides to the story as far as I was concerned.

My mother was deeply hurt when she found and read a copy of my report. To be judged harshly—and inaccurately, I now know—by her son was a difficult and hurtful thing. She asked me to sit down with her to discuss it, which we did. I can only regret that she didn't live long enough for me to fully recant my thoughts, but it taught me an important lesson. Words once uttered—even when prompted by temporary emotion—are hard to ever fully take back. And sometimes life doesn't give you a chance.

By the time my father dropped out of the 1976 presidential race in March, I'd already taken the spring semester off and wasn't due back at school until the fall. My mother had recently been impressed by a young man she knew who'd gone to sea, so she encouraged me to do the same. I liked the idea. It seemed an appealingly exotic undertaking and a way to make some money and see some sights. I took a job as a deck hand on what was at the time a very modern container ship called the *Resource*, which traveled from Port Elizabeth, New Jersey, to Portsmouth, Virginia, to Rotterdam, Holland (the world's largest port), then to Bremerhaven, Germany. I don't remember how much I made that summer, but it seemed to add up pretty quickly since there was no place to spend the money at sea.

The boatswain knew who my father was, but I didn't advertise my family background to the rest of the crew. I was, at twenty, the youngest guy on the ship. The next oldest guy was close to thirty, and everybody else was at least forty. I could tell from the way they looked at me what they were thinking: "Why is this kid going off to sea?" But they were mostly glad to see that a young guy was interested in this line of work to which they'd devoted their lives. Even then, theirs was a shrinking profession, due to competition from foreign ships. In addition, the nomadic existence was hard on the crewmen's families—if they had families at all. (The ship's officers tended to be family men—the first officer had wives in New Jersey *and* Holland—but the crew consisted mostly of bachelors.)

As a deck hand, one of my jobs was to stand watch eight hours a day, and since I was the youngest, I got the least desirable watch hours. My shifts went from midnight to 4 A.M. and then from noon to 4 P.M. With my nights all chopped up, I never got much sleep— not more than three or four hours at a time, which turned out to be good practice for tending to two infants later in life. Most days, I'd work twelve hours instead of the required eight, because aside from reading the books I'd brought along, there wasn't much to do except eat, listen to the shortwave radio, or look out to sea. After my nighttime watch shift ended, I'd grab a few hours sleep, shave, then report to the boatswain around eight o'clock to see what needed to be done that day.

The watchman was responsible for looking out for the lights of other ships. It was a pretty antiquated job, considering that the *Resource* had a computer navigation system with satellite technology that kept the captain informed on the location of other ships. I guess the theory was, if the computer system broke, you'd have a pair of eyes on deck to fall back on. Standing outside the bridge in the misty North Atlantic night was a chilly task. Even with several layers of clothes on, I could feel the damp, icy wind against my skin.

My watch partner, Clarence Owens, was from Colorado. He had no teeth, no hair, and tattoos on almost every part of his body. He used to drink a fifth of Seagram's VO and at least a couple of six-packs every day. It was quite remarkable to me that he still managed to do his job, but he did. I didn't see much of Clarence when we were on watch, because we worked in two-hour shifts. While I was on watch, he'd be down in the break room grabbing a nap, eating, listening to the radio, and probably warming himself with whisky. I did see him during the workday, though, when we were assigned projects together—inspecting the stacks, picking up the pilot, letting go the pilot, docking, untying the ship when we were leaving port. I remember once when I was over the side of the ship, tying up the gangway and eyeing the icy water below.

"Kid, you know what the life expectancy in the North Sea is?" Clarence said.

I said that I did not.

"Well, you get hypothermia after about three and a half minutes. You know how long it takes to stop this ship?"

"No, how long?"

"Half an hour. So if you fall overboard, don't worry about us coming back, because you'd be dead by then, if the propeller hasn't already turned you into shark bait."

"Thanks, Clarence," I said, tightening my grip on the railing. "That's very reassuring."

8
MY MOTHER'S DEATH

*Maybe it's because I was an only child, or maybe it's
because I was naïve or in denial or that I'm an
optimist by nature, but I had never seriously
contemplated her mortality.*

WHEN THE *RESOURCE* returned to the States after five weeks at sea,
I came back to Washington and worked as a waiter at the Hyatt
Regency until school started. Even though I'd taken a semester off
to work on my father's campaign, I still had enough credits that I
was able to graduate on time in the spring of 1978, earning a degree
in business economics and public policy, with honors, from IU's
business school. That January, just as I was beginning the last
semester of my senior year, my mother went for her three-times-a-
year checkup and learned that her cancer was back. She told me
when I came home to visit in March. This time it was spreading
throughout her whole body, and the prognosis wasn't good. I stayed
home that summer, spending time with my mother and interning
as an assistant economist in the Antitrust Division of the Justice
Department. Even with her illness, she insisted that I start law
school on time, but before I began my studies at the University of

Virginia that fall, she took me on a cruise of the Scandinavian countries, the land of her mother's ancestors—a trip she'd always wanted us to make. Some of my earliest memories are of my maternal grandmother speaking to me in fluent Norwegian. Going back to my mother's roots made us both feel better. It was a special time.

Even though I knew she was sick again, her death still came as a tremendous shock to me. The last time I spoke with her was two weeks before she died, at our home in Washington. It was a very emotional visit. She was having trouble breathing by then, and I remember sitting at her bedside in the darkened room as she told me how much I meant to her, how proud she was of me. She said that her two biggest regrets were that she would never meet the girl I would marry, and that she'd never get to see her grandchildren. Now those are my regrets. When I think about her never having had a chance to know Susan and the boys, I feel a tremendous emptiness. The boys and I have planted a magnolia tree—her favorite—in the yard at our house, and I tell them stories about her so they'll know who she was and what she was like, but it will never be the same as them knowing her. I'm just grateful Nick and Beau have had a chance to know their other grandparents, as well as Jane, who's been a surrogate grandmother to them.

When I said good-bye to my mother after that visit, it was pretty clear that she thought she wasn't going to live. I saw her once more, out at the National Cancer Institute in Bethesda, Maryland, but she was on a respirator by then. She couldn't talk, and she was in and out of consciousness. As I was sitting with her, she got tears in her eyes and squeezed my hand with what was left of her strength. A few days later, as I was studying for final exams at my apartment in Charlottesville, Jane Sinnenberg called with the news that my mother had passed away. She was forty-six years old.

Her death hit me very hard. Maybe it's because I was an only child, or maybe it's because I was naive or in denial or that I'm an optimist by nature, but I had never seriously contemplated her mortality. I always knew she'd recover, just knew it. Now, one of the permanent anchors in my life, a given, was gone. My father was devastated, too. She'd been not only his wife, but also his political partner, actively involved in all aspects of his life.

The National Cathedral was filled with people for her memorial service—it was really quite an honor. A second service was held in Terre Haute at Centenary Methodist Church, and I was moved by the tremendous outpouring there as well. Afterwards, my father and I spent a few days together in Florida, just to walk on the beach, be together. In retrospect, I'm afraid I didn't fully appreciate the void that had been created in his life, the loneliness, loss of love. Even at twenty-three, I don't think it occurred to me that a parent could have such feelings. But as an adult and parent myself now, of course I know.

After Florida, I returned to Charlottesville to finish my exams, but it was hard to concentrate on school. What I needed was an escape, some time to get away from it all. I decided to go to Europe with Larry Ceisler, a friend of mine I'd met when we were laying railroad track on the Metro. That summer, Renault was offering unlimited mileage on a rental car in Europe, and we intended to take full advantage. We flew to England and boarded the ferry to Calais, where we picked up the car and then drove all over Europe, down the west coast of France, through Spain, back up to Monaco, then to Paris, Luxembourg, southern Germany, Austria, Hungary, and Yugoslavia. In Greece, we asked a college student to return the car to France, and, amazingly enough, she did.

I was trying to work a lot of pain and anger out of my system during that trip, and I'm afraid I wasn't the best traveling companion.

Each morning I woke up feeling like I had a huge hole inside me. The healthy thing would probably have been to embrace that feeling and come to terms with it, let it all hang out, but I was raised to be more stoic, part of my mother's Scandinavian heritage perhaps. My way of dealing with tremendous sadness was to avoid it, and I ended up just letting it sit there inside me for years.

The whole experience also tested my faith. Why does a child die? Why does your mother pass away in the prime of her life with everything to live for? My mom had been very devout, and in the months following her death, I kept a Bible beside my bed at law school and read a passage every night before going to sleep. I kept looking for answers, but eventually I began to believe that there aren't any answers. I think you just have to hold onto your faith, trust in God, and accept the fact that some tragedies are simply beyond our understanding and control. These days, what mystifies me are the human tragedies that *are* within our control.

Despite the difficult circumstances, that trip to Europe nevertheless proved to be a broadening experience for me and one I think my mother would have appreciated. Travel had always been very important to her—the *most* important thing after family, according to one of her journal entries in 1970. It offered her a chance to relax, a chance to learn about other people and places. She traveled across the country in her work for the American Cancer Society and around the world in her trips with my father. She made sure that I traveled, too. In addition to our visit to Scandinavia, she'd taken me on a two-week driving tour of the British Isles in 1970, a trip we made with Jane and Steven Sinnenberg. The year before, a political visit to Russia had doubled as our family vacation. Since those early trips, I've tried to learn about our diverse nation and world, and it's important to me that my sons do, too. I especially want them to acquire an understanding of our increasingly interconnected world, to appreciate other cultures and languages. Twenty years from now, I expect fluency in Spanish to be a prerequisite for success in the U.S. and a knowledge of other nations' economies, history, and politics to be equally important.

After my trip to Europe, I came back to law school in the fall, studied for a year, then took the next fall semester off to serve as the campaign chairman for my father's last senatorial bid, an election he lost to Dan Quayle, then a U.S. congressman from northeast Indiana. Nineteen-eighty was a landslide year for the Republican Party, thanks largely to a floundering economy. Today it's hard to imagine what it was like, with unemployment at 11 or 12 percent, inflation close to 20 percent, and interest rates at 22 or 23 percent. To make matters worse, the anniversary of the hostage crisis fell one day prior to Election Day. Following a revolution in Iran, students had seized the American embassy in Tehran on November 4, 1979. They were holding about a hundred American hostages, and President Carter had been unable to win their release in the wake of a botched rescue attempt. With the hostage crisis and the poor economy dominating the public's consciousness, the Carter administration was vulnerable. People wanted a change, and the legislative branch was not exempt. My father lost, winning 46 percent of the votes to Qualye's 54 percent.

Those were hard times for him, with the election defeat coming just two years after my mother died. Losing an election is nothing compared to losing a family member, but it did mean that the career in public service he'd pursued for twenty-six years suddenly came to an end, and he had sixty days to figure out what else he was going to do with his life. He also had to work through the feelings that any public official experiences after being voted out of office, feelings that verge on rejection. Getting voted out is, of course, an occupational hazard, part of the democratic process, but it takes a certain amount of detachment to embrace that conclusion.

Since then, he's been practicing law, and he's still going strong at seventy-five. I think his work ethic stems from his rural roots and the satisfaction he derives from accomplishments, preferably to something greater than self. He wouldn't be happy if he weren't active, making a contribution in the world. After he retired from politics, he opened a law firm in Indiana but eventually joined a firm in Washington. He stays busy, gets to Indiana every few weeks, and is active with some of the issues he championed in public life. If he could be doing anything he wanted, I think he'd like to teach at one of the universities in Indiana and raise livestock. His life hasn't worked out that way, but I believe those are still his two loves—teaching young people and working the land.

These days we see each other every couple of months, and he's able to spend some time with the boys. He also remarried, to the former Kitty Halpin, and has another son, my half-brother Christopher, who's now an undergraduate at IU. Christopher's a wonderful young man, and Susan and I had him up to our home in Indianapolis a couple of times, but distance and a twenty-five-year age difference have kept the two of us from being as close as I'd like.

I was born on
December 26, 1955, in
Shirkieville, Indiana,
near Terre Haute.

A more formal portrait with
my parents, around 1958.

Under the careful supervision of my parents, I "drove" a tractor for the first time in July 1957 on our family farm at Shirkieville.

An IU cowboy, April 1960. We lived in Bloomington while my mother attended college at Indiana University and my father went to law school.

With my parents,
around 1962.

My mother, Marvella, was an amazing
and accomplished woman. One thing she
instilled in me was a love of reading—a
passion Susan and I try to pass along to
our boys.

I spent four great summers at Culver
Military Academy in Culver, Indiana.
By my third year, 1969, I had plenty of
badges to decorate my uniform.

With my parents, I attended the Democratic nominating convention at the State Fairgrounds Coliseum, June 1962. Dad won the nomination and was elected to the U.S. Senate in November.

On the campaign trail with Dad at the 1968 Indiana State Fair.

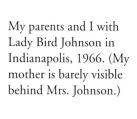

My parents and I with Lady Bird Johnson in Indianapolis, 1966. (My mother is barely visible behind Mrs. Johnson.)

9

My Father's Politics

Sometimes people aske me how a "liberal"
politician like my dad came out of 1950s Indiana.

My FATHER ONCE told a reporter for *The New York Times* that he thought I took the loss to Quayle even harder than he did, and maybe that's true. I think it's always harder to see a loved one disappointed than it is to be disappointed yourself. I know how lousy I'd feel if one of my children were unsuccessful at something he really wanted to do. After the 1980 election, I came close to being disillusioned by the political process, because I believed in my father and what he was trying to do, and yet he was defeated. "How could this happen?" I wondered. But now, with the benefit of experience and the perspective age brings, I understand the respect for others and the appreciation for diversity of opinion that democracy requires. Voters have a right to express their views, and you have to respect them even if they don't coincide with your own. I don't dwell on that defeat anymore. My father had a long and successful career in public service, and that's a lot to be grateful for.

My father's politics also made him a rather controversial figure, a fact I first became aware of during his campaign for the U.S.

Senate in 1962, when I was in second grade. Some of the children at school had a little chant: "Birch Bayh, he's a rat, 'cause he is a Demo-crat." It sounds pretty funny now, but when you're six or seven and kids on the playground are singing mean songs about your father, it hurts.

The stakes were even higher once my father made a name for himself in Washington. In 1968, on the day that Bobby Kennedy was shot, a man phoned my father and said that the Ku Klux Klan would kill him when he spoke that evening at a scheduled appearance in Whiting, a town in northwest Indiana. My father also ended up on Nixon's enemies list for opposing two of the president's Supreme Court nominations. After my father led the Senate's defeat of Judge G. Harrold Carswell's nomination in April 1970, CBS news commentator Eric Sevareid likened him to a "Midwestern John F. Kennedy" on the evening news. When I answered the phone later that night, a man on the other end said, "You tell your father that if he is going to be a Midwestern John F. Kennedy, I am going to be another Lee Harvey Oswald."

That phone call scared me, but it never dawned on me that something could actually happen to my dad. Once I got older and understood that my father wasn't invincible, I just came to terms with the fact. If you're involved in public life, controversy is part of the territory. A leader is defined not only by his friends, but by his enemies as well. It's far better to take on risks and fight for things you believe in than to stand safely for nothing at all.

Later on, when I was volunteering for my father's campaigns, he'd sometimes get heckled during a parade, or while he was meeting voters at a factory's gate. Such activities are an essential part of being a good public official. They give you a chance to get out and see people, hear what's on their minds, and let them see you. But you're also a sitting duck for occasional verbal abuse.

It wasn't easy to listen to them heckling my father, but now that I'm the one who occasionally gets heckled, I understand that you just have to have a thick skin. For me, that's easier said than done. I can walk in a parade where everybody is cheering and applauding, and at the end, I'll turn to one of my staff members and ask them, "What do you think was bothering that one guy back there who was booing?" So far the twins haven't had a chance to hear me get heckled, but I suspect that someday they probably will. I only hope that they'll understand that the right to free speech is one of the things that makes our country great. Even though I don't like to be booed any more than the next guy does, I think it's a good thing that you *can* boo a U.S. senator. Besides, the vast majority of people couldn't be nicer—even those who disagree with me on issues or policies.

Sometimes people ask me how a "liberal" politician like my dad came out of 1950s Indiana. The bottom line is, I don't know. But I've got a few thoughts on the topic. First, I don't think my father was perceived by voters as being as liberal early in his career as he was later on, and I think that perception is fair. He was well within the philosophical mainstream of the state when he was first elected in the 1950s. But as the fifties gave way to the sixties, society was changing. People wanted civil rights for minorities, equal treatment for women, protection for our environment, and progress on a host of other issues. And as my father took up the great causes of his time, his views evolved over the course of his life in public service, reflecting both his sense of right and wrong and the era in which he lived.

Second, whether you consider my father a liberal depends on how you define the term. Compared to some who followed, he was fiscally *conservative*. He never voted for budget deficits as large as those passed by Congress in later years.

People frequently ask me about the differences in our approach to public policy issues. My father is remembered as a Great Society liberal, whereas I'm seen as more moderate, even conservative in some areas—a "genuinely fiscally conservative Democrat" as *The Wall Street Journal* once put it. I think part of the difference can be attributed to the changing times. The world is a different place today. In the early sixties, people weren't so concerned about fiscal rectitude and balancing budgets. These days we're more conscientious about not running up big debts, because we've seen the kind of damage that sizable, long-term deficits can do to the economy.

Also, in the fifties and sixties, the United States really had no economic competition. In those faraway days before globalization, we could produce just about anything and it would sell. "Made in Japan" connoted cheaply made goods, trinkets in Cracker Jack boxes. Now Japan and a host of other countries are producing high-quality, low-cost products that provide strong competition for American-made goods. Technological advances and the substitution of capital for labor have transformed entire sectors of the economy. And so we take prosperity for granted at our own peril and must focus intently on what makes the United States competitive, what creates jobs, how we promote growth.

In a nutshell, the world today is different from what it was thirty or forty years ago. My father and I share the same values, but the way we implement those values, give them currency and meaning in the context of our times, will of course be different. And that's natural, to be expected.

The world certainly looks a lot different when it comes to families in the United States. Since 1960, when my father was a member of the Indiana state legislature, the number of families without a father present in the home has more than doubled, to about 40 percent. I generally think our country is moving forward, making progress, but when it comes to families and fathers, the outlook isn't as bright. Whether my father would be championing responsible fatherhood if he were in the Senate today, I can't say. However, I do think he'd be involved in any effort that he felt would help children, especially disadvantaged kids, and, regrettably, they're the ones hurt most by the dramatic changes sweeping over American families and the irresponsible behavior of too many men.

10

FALLING IN LOVE

To hear Susan tell it, I was just looking for a safe
date and figured she was the kind of girl who
wouldn't wear a lampshade on her head.

SUSAN AND I met in the summer of 1981, but our mothers actually met years earlier at the 1968 Democratic Convention in Chicago—one of the few good things to come out of that particular convention. Susan's mother, Carol, had been active on Bobby Kennedy's campaign and was in Chicago with the California delegation. She and my mother struck up a friendship and continued to correspond in the following years. Later, my mother introduced Carol to Jane Sinnenberg, and Carol and Jane maintained their friendship after my mother died.

When Susan graduated from the University of California at Berkeley in 1981, she landed an internship in Washington with U.S. Congressman Pete Stark, a Democrat representing California. Jane offered to put her up for the summer. I was still in law school and was working that summer as an intern at a big international firm in Washington.

Jane kept inviting me to dinner. "There's this really nice girl staying with us," she said. "You've got to come meet her."

"Right, right, right," I said. I figured "nice girl" meant "sews her own clothes." Fortunately, Jane persisted, and eventually I went over for dinner.

Even though our mothers had been friends, Susan and I had never met, but I'd probably seen her on TV without realizing it. She'd been a cheerleader at the University of California, Berkeley, at the time I was in law school. After a late night of studying, I'd often relax with my friends by turning on the TV at eleven-thirty or twelve. Back then, ESPN frequently broadcast West Coast games at that hour, so I ended up watching Cal now and then, and when the cameras panned to the cheerleaders, I probably caught a glimpse or two of my future wife. (Later on, I mentioned to Susan the names of a few Cal players I remembered, and she confirmed that they were on the team when she was a cheerleader.)

Jane and her husband, Bob, lived in an apartment in Roslyn, Virginia, overlooking the Potomac River and Georgetown. It was just the four of us at dinner that night. Even then, I think Jane must have wanted Susan and me to get together. She cooked a terrific Italian meal and sat us across from one another. After dinner, Susan and I ended up on the balcony, talking about her courses at Cal and looking at the lights of the Washington skyline. I didn't have contact lenses in those days, and I'd been too vain to wear my glasses, so I spent much of the evening trying to get a good look at Susan. It quite literally was not "love at first sight." I suspected she was very pretty, but I couldn't be sure. It didn't matter, though. I already knew I wanted to ask her out. Though I tend to be somewhat reserved, I've always liked people who are upbeat and outgoing. Susan's vivaciousness was the first thing about her that impressed me. I also liked her sense of humor, her optimism, and the fact that she was obviously very smart. I remember thinking that she seemed to be everything that I wanted in a woman, and, as it turns out, I was right.

I called her a few weeks later and invited her to the law firm's big social event of the season, a cookout at one of the partner's summer homes. To hear Susan tell it, I was just looking for a safe date and figured she was the kind of girl who wouldn't wear a lampshade on her head. Truth was, I was already smitten. She turned a lot of heads that night, especially mine (and this time I was wearing my glasses).

A few days later, we went on our first real date—dinner at Martin's, a restaurant in Georgetown. Afterward, I suggested we go for ice cream. As Susan would soon learn, a love of ice cream is part of my family's genetic code. (In 1968, when Hubert Humphrey chose Ed Muskie for his vice-presidential running mate instead of my father, my dad went back to his hotel room and ordered twelve scoops of chocolate ice cream.) Susan and I went to a place called Steve's and got a cup of vanilla with M&Ms mixed in, then walked up a quiet side street until we found some steps where we could sit down and talk. Before long, a calico alley cat came along and took an interest in our ice cream, and we ended up sharing it with her. She was very happy that night; we were very happy that night.

But our relationship faced some practical obstacles. At the end of the summer Susan had to return to California to start law school at USC, and I had to go back to Charlottesville. In January, after I finished my degree, I moved to Indianapolis for a year and a half to clerk for a federal judge (a wonderful man named Jim Noland), then took three months off, loaded up a backpack and duffel bag, and embarked on another trip—this time all the way around the world.

I left Indianapolis and flew to Oklahoma City to see my cousins, then to Los Angeles to visit a friend. Susan and I had been talking on the phone every now and then, so while I was in L.A., I asked her out. She already had a date, but she promptly called him and said she was sick so she could spend the evening with me.

From Los Angeles, I traveled to Japan for a couple of weeks, then Hong Kong, Singapore, Thailand, and Sri Lanka, sending Susan postcards from each stop. I wanted to go to Kenya next, but I got a mean case of dysentery in Kandy, Sri Lanka, where I was visiting the Temple of the Tooth, which, according to legend, housed one of the Buddha's teeth—at least it did before the Portuguese arrived in the 1500s, took whatever was there, and threw it into the Indian Ocean. The dysentery really knocked the wind out of my sails, so instead of going to Africa, I flew to Athens. Compared to where I'd been, Greece was like coming home to Indianapolis. I stayed a couple of weeks, then headed to Italy and made a brief stop in Holland. England was next, and then I finished the trip in Scotland, where I met up with two of my best friends from law school to play golf.

It wasn't until Susan and I both returned to Washington that we started to date seriously. After my trip, I went to work full-time for the D.C. law firm where I'd interned. I knew I eventually wanted to go home to Indiana, but I thought it would be good to establish myself professionally in a top firm where my family wasn't as well known. That fall, during her third year of law school at USC, Susan came to Washington on an internship to clerk for a judge.

One afternoon, I was driving through Georgetown when a girl on the sidewalk caught my eye. "Boy," I said to myself, "that's a really cute girl." The girl was giving me the same kind of look. It was a moment before Susan and I recognized each other. That's when we realized that we might have met even if Jane hadn't introduced us, though it would have been much more awkward. Still, we like to think fate played a role. Susan returned to USC at the end of the semester, and during the next six months, we visited one another and racked up some big phone bills. On one trip to Los Angeles, I accidentally left my running shoes behind. A few days later, I got a package in the mail—my shoes, filled with Hershey's kisses.

That spring, Susan graduated from law school, but she was still one course shy of fulfilling her degree requirements. She'd been putting herself through school as a waitress and couldn't afford another semester at USC, so she returned to Washington and took family law at Catholic University. After she passed the bar exam, she celebrated with a vacation in Europe, and I arranged to meet her in Rome for the last few days of her trip. By this time, we'd already considered the idea of getting married. We'd also talked about life in the public eye, the ways in which my father's career had affected my mother and me. I knew that I eventually wanted to run for office, and having grown up in a high-profile family, I realized public life wasn't for everybody.

I decided to pop the question in Rome, but I almost didn't get the chance. A few days before our rendezvous, Susan was hit by a car while riding a bicycle in Austria. She was taken to the hospital but suffered only scrapes and bruises. We were very lucky.

When I arrived in Italy, I was pretty nervous. I'd had serious girlfriends before Susan, but I'd never come close to marriage. I figured I needed all the help I could get, so I took her to the most romantic place I could find: the Scalinata Spagna (or "Spanish Steps"), a giant marble staircase that leads from the French church Trinità dei Monti down to the Piazza di Spagna and its boat-shaped fountain, the Barcaccia. In the 1700s, beautiful men and women would gather at the steps in hopes of being chosen as an artist's model. As we were strolling the piazza, I pulled a large, rectangular, gift-wrapped box from my backpack.

"Dear, I have something for you," I said.

Susan looked at the box. "Shoes?" she asked, clearly disappointed.

"Open it and see," I said. And so she opened the box to find a smaller one inside, and then another and another. The last box held an engagement ring. I asked her to marry me, and she said yes on the spot.

11
A YOUNG FAMILY

When you're on your deathbed looking back on your
life, you probably won't regret that you didn't spend
more time at the office, but you'll certainly regret not
getting to know your children as well as you wanted to.

AFTER WE CAME back to the States, Susan settled down to work at
the Washington office of one of California's most prestigious firms.
By that time, I was eager to return home. In the fall of 1984, I took
a leave of absence from the law firm to volunteer on Wayne
Townsend's gubernatorial campaign in Indiana. After the election,
I came back to Washington, put my affairs in order, and moved to
Indianapolis. Susan was still in D.C., working at the law firm and
planning our wedding. We were married on the morning of April
13, 1985, in the grand choir chapel the National Cathedral. There
were three hundred guests, mostly personal friends from
Washington and Indiana, people we'd known for a long time. We
had an afternoon reception at the Washington Club on Dupont
Circle, and then we spent our wedding night at the Hay-Adams
Hotel, across the street from the White House. The next morning
we left for a weeklong honeymoon in the Caribbean—a couple of

days in St. Martin, then five days in St. Bart's. At that point, Susan needed the honeymoon more than I did. She'd been planning the wedding for months, whereas all I had to do was fly into town, survive my bachelor party, and show up at the church.

After the honeymoon, Susan moved to Indianapolis and practiced law with Barnes & Thornburg. I was practicing with my father's firm, and after he moved, I went with Bingham Summers Welsh & Spilman.

The following year, I decided to run for secretary of state. Not surprisingly, my father's choice of careers influenced mine to some degree. I was always interested in public policy and politics, because that's what we talked about around the dinner table when I was growing up. If my family had talked about engineering or business or farming, perhaps I would have been more interested in one of those occupations. I admired both of my parents and what they were trying to do for our state and country. They helped me see public service as a noble calling.

But I wasn't one of those kids who, in seventh grade, was saying, "Here's my plan to be president of the United States." Nor did I ever feel a need to go into politics simply because it's something that my father had done. I could have been happy doing other things. If I'd lost that first election and never gone on to hold any other public office, I wouldn't have felt unfulfilled. My father's career has really helped me keep life in perspective. I learned from his experience that there are worse things that can happen to you than losing an election—a lot worse. When you go into politics, you leave office only one of three ways: you retire, you're defeated, or you die. If you think about it in those terms, losing an election isn't so bad.

Fortunately, I won the election and became Indiana's secretary of state in 1986 at age thirty. My opponent was Rob Bowen, the son of former two-term governor Otis Bowen who'd gone on to become secretary of health and human services under Ronald Reagan.

Two years later, in 1988, I ran for governor against Republican Lieutenant Governor John Mutz. I campaigned on a platform of fiscal responsibility, opposing higher taxes and bloated bureaucracies and criticizing as excessive financial incentives given an automobile company to locate in state. This time, with the help of a wonderful staff—Joe Hogsett, Bill Moreau, Les Miller, Sally Kirkpatrick, Mary Finnegan, Phil Schermerhorn, Bill Stinson, and Fred Glass, to name only a few, plus other supporters and volunteers too numerous to mention—I managed 53 percent of the vote, becoming Indiana's first Democratic governor in twenty years. I was elected at age thirty-two, sworn in at thirty-three, and for six years was the youngest governor in the country. In 1992, I was reelected by a 63–37 margin over Attorney General Linley Pearson.

Susan's professional life has undergone a good deal of upheaval thanks to my political career. When I became secretary of state, her job in the area of securities and corporate law represented a potential conflict of interest, because the secretary of state oversees the securities division. To avoid any problems, she moved into the area of utility regulatory law. But then I was elected governor, and the governor appoints the utility regulatory commission, so to avoid another potential conflict of interest, she went to work in Eli Lilly's federal regulatory section, where she dealt only with the federal government and had nothing to do with the state government. In her five years at Lilly, she became very knowledgeable about FDA regulatory compliance issues.

In 1994, President Clinton appointed her to the International Joint Commission, which deals with environmental issues between Canada and the U.S., principally on the Great Lakes. During his final two years in office, she was confidentially approached about the possibility of a high-profile position in the White House, but because of the extraordinary demands of the job and the boys' tender age, she demurred. She has also taught environmental law in the business program at Butler University and has worked as a special correspondent for WISH-TV, Indianapolis' CBS affiliate, hosting a weekly segment on family and parenting issues.

These days, Susan works at home, serving on several corporate boards and managing a speakers program at Butler University, where she also sits on the board of trustees. Some people would say she's made sacrifices for my career, but Susan doesn't look at it that way. She views life as a series of doors: when some shut, others open. Had I not gone into politics, she might have ended up happy as a partner at a law firm, but she says she's more happy now that she's able to work part-time and spend much of each day with the boys, who are her top priority.

The twins were about fourteen months old when I finished my second term as governor. I was proud of what I'd accomplished in those eight years: the single largest tax cut in state history; the biggest budget surplus in state history; national leadership in moving people from welfare to work; more dollars for schools every year; higher academic standards for students in kindergarten through twelfth grade and new college opportunities; more than 375,000 new jobs; tougher laws against crime; and improved environmental quality. Most of all, I was proud of becoming a father, and I was looking forward to spending some time out of the limelight with Susan and the boys.

We loved the Meridian-Kessler neighborhood where the governor's residence is located, so that fall, we began shopping for a house in the area. There wasn't much on the market at that time of year, but we were lucky to find a place we liked that was in our price range, a house at Forty-ninth Street and Washington Boulevard. We moved in January of 1997 and lived at 4821 Washington Boulevard for two years, until I was elected to the Senate. During those two years, Susan was teaching at Butler University as a distinguished visiting professor of environmental policy and business law, and serving on the International Joint Commission (a job she held until President Bush was elected and replaced the Clinton appointees with his own). I was teaching at IU's Kelley School of Business, practicing law, and eventually campaigning for the Senate. It was a busy time, but since I didn't have to travel as much as I had when I was governor—or as much as I do now—I was home with the boys a lot.

I'm very grateful for those two years. "Take time to smell the roses" is inscribed on a clock in my office—one of my mother's favorite sayings. I'm very good at looking at that inscription and not very good at living by it, but I try to when it comes to the boys. As I used to tell my students at IU, when you're on your deathbed looking back on your life, you probably won't regret that you didn't spend more time at the office, but you'll certainly regret not getting to know your children as well as you wanted to.

As you'd expect, our house on Washington Boulevard was more modest than the governor's residence, but it was enough for us, and we enjoyed the privacy and rhythm of a more normal life. At the governor's residence, with its security guards and constant stream of visitors, there was always somebody around. Now, for the first time in eight years, we were alone in a house, just the four of us.

I remember going for a run on the day we moved in. When I was governor, the state police had always been with me, following at a discreet distance, but now here I was, running along Washington Boulevard, all by myself. After all those years of never really being alone, it took me a little while to get used to that feeling. Some states continue to provide security for six months after the governor leaves office, but in Indiana, the police protection ends on the day you leave office. After I went to Frank O'Bannon's swearing in, a state trooper drove me to an automobile dealership where I bought a car then drove home. It was my first significant driving in eight years. A new menace had been unleashed upon our unsuspecting motoring public.

That winter, we'd bundle up the boys, strap them into their double stroller, and take long walks through the Meridian-Kessler and Butler-Tarkington neighborhoods, crisscrossing the Butler University campus and admiring the grand historic homes up and down Meridian Street. The stroller was a side-by-side model, rather than front-and-back, because we didn't want either of the boys to feel like he was taking a backseat.

Since their birth had been such a public event, passersby would occasionally stop us on the street to chat. Most just wanted to know how the boys were doing, and I felt honored that people took such an interest in them. As the weather warmed up, we spent time playing on the swing set in the backyard, and then we'd go up the street to Friendly's, where Nick and Beau could barely peek over the counter as they ate their ice cream. On rainy Saturdays or Sundays, we made a bee line for the Children's Museum; on sunny days, we headed to the zoo.

Now and then, one of the boys would come down with a mild cold or an ear infection—the usual stuff—but mostly they were healthy and happy. Nick did give us a scare, though. One morning, before he'd learned to ride a tricycle, he was pushing himself along the driveway on a plastic toy worm with wheels. He came to an abrupt stop near the sidewalk and toppled headfirst over the handlebars onto his face. It was very traumatic—for him and for us. He scraped his nose and lip and chipped a front tooth, which ended up developing an abscess and eventually had to be pulled. Until his adult tooth grew in to fill the gap, I could always get him to smile by calling him Snaggle Tooth.

Though we'd taken the boys to Hilton Head and Chicago when I was governor, it was during our time on Washington Boulevard that we really began to learn the joys of traveling with young children. Our first beginner's mistake came when the boys were about two years old. We thought it would be fun to go on a family ski trip to Colorado with Susan's mom. The possibility of altitude sickness never occurred to us, but sure enough, both boys ended up with flu-like symptoms and were very cranky for our whole stay in Colorado. The flight back to Indiana wasn't much better. We thought we were doing well when we managed to secure the last row of seats on the plane, right next to the bathroom, but as soon as we settled in, Beau got sick to his stomach and vomited all down my back. I didn't have a clean shirt in my carry-on bag, so I sat there for the two-and-a-half-hour flight. The aroma didn't exactly endear me to the other passengers. Things got worse when I let Nick bring his prized toy car into the airplane bathroom. As I finished changing his diaper—an ordeal in the cramped quarters that seemed to last an eternity—I handed the car back to him and whoosh, out of his hands it went, right down the toilet. Nick was distraught. He wanted me to retrieve his car, but I was reluctant to stick my hand down that toilet, past the silver trap door. It was a moment of truth. Nick looked at me with a pleading expression; I looked at him with a pleading expression.

I ended up buying him a new toy car.

12

A SECOND SENATOR BAYH

Crossing the state line felt like a watershed moment:
I was heading to Washington to occupy the Senate
seat my father had held for eighteen years.

AFTER I LEFT the governorship, I began laying the groundwork for a run for the United States Senate—raising money, maintaining political ties, working on public-policy positions. I announced my candidacy in early 1998 with a fly-around tour of the state, starting in Indianapolis and stopping at campaign rallies in Fort Wayne, South Bend, Lake County, Terre Haute, Evansville, and Jeffersonville all in one day. I was unopposed in the Democratic primary; the Republicans had a three-way contest won by Paul Helmke, then the mayor of Fort Wayne. Though I enjoyed a sizable lead from the outset, I wasn't taking anything for granted. That was the year of Monica Lewinsky, a scandal I thought created the potential for an adverse reaction against Democrats, especially in a state like Indiana. Even so, I ended up with 64 percent of the vote, which was more than I'd expected.

Compared to my father's Senate campaigns, mine was very

expensive—about $3.9 million—an unfortunate fact of politics today. The worst things about fund-raising are all the time it takes, time that could more usefully be devoted to addressing society's challenges, and the perception that money influences public decisions, a belief that understandably alienates many people. The problem is driven in large part by the cost of television advertising, which keeps going up. The vast majority of Americans today get their information from TV. So, if you don't communicate in that medium, most of the public won't know what you stand for. Also, with a hundred channels to choose from, the audience is much more fragmented now. In the old days, when there were three networks, a candidate could reach everybody by advertising on only three channels. These days, you have to run many more ads on many more channels for anybody to see them.

On the plus side, there are a lot more split-ticket voters now than in my father's time. The largest group of voters today isn't Democrats or Republicans, it's independents. I think voters are more willing to look at a candidate, assess his or her qualifications and ideas, and vote accordingly, rather than adhering strictly to partisanship and ideology. Most people don't care as much about right or left as they do about what's right or wrong, what works, what makes sense. I've always felt I could do well in such an electoral environment because I approach issues from a pragmatic rather than an ideological perspective.

By the fall of 1998, the fatherhood movement was gathering momentum. On November 4, 1998, the day after Election Day, a landmark three-day fatherhood conference opened at Morehouse College in Atlanta. The Morehouse Conference on African-American Fathers focused on the fatherlessness epidemic in the

African-American community, in which the consequences of father absence have been felt most significantly.

The conference identified the problem of father absence as our country's next great civil rights challenge. "We call upon all African-American leaders to bring to this movement the same energy and dedication, the same passion and fearlessness, and the same creativity and courage that was summoned to wage the struggle for basic civil rights," the conference organizers declared in a written call to action. "And we call upon our national, state, and municipal leaders to put the full weight of government resource at all levels . . . behind partnerships designed to reunite fathers with their children and to strengthen families."

According to research presented at the conference, 70 percent of African-American children were born to unmarried mothers at the time, and at least 80 percent of African-American children could expect to spend a significant portion of their childhood separated from their fathers. The low marriage rate is the primary reason many children don't have more contact with their fathers. In many cases, though, mothers, regardless of race, don't *want* to marry the fathers of their children, because the men aren't good marriage prospects.

Sadly, too many men die young, end up in jail, or become addicted to drugs. The low employment rate among black men is a big factor, too. Not surprisingly, an unwed mother is three times more likely to want to marry the father of her children if he has a job. As Columbia Professor Ron Mincy, himself an African American, is fond of saying, "We need more BMWs—Black Men Working." But the epidemic of father absence was by no means a black problem. In fact, among all groups, the percentage of father-absent children was rising fastest among whites, and the trend lines suggested that America as a whole would soon reflect the experience of the African-American community.

Though I'd been out of public office for two years, I'd nevertheless spent much of that time actively involved in fatherhood issues—namely, raising Nick and Beau. Now I was looking forward to promoting responsible fatherhood as a member of the Senate. Two months after the election, Susan, the boys, and I left our home and headed to Washington, D.C. I'll never forget the trip. We'd been planning to make the drive on January 2, but a huge blizzard was rolling in from the west, so we decided to leave on New Year's Day instead, hoping to beat the weather. We woke before dawn and tucked the boys into their car seats with blankets so they could sleep during the trip. I remember driving east on I-70 with the sun rising ahead of us, a bright pink sky over a frozen Indiana landscape of corn fields and farmhouses. Crossing the state line felt like a watershed moment: I was heading to Washington to occupy the Senate seat my father had held for eighteen years.

I didn't make a very grand arrival in D.C., though. When we pulled into town after twelve hours of driving, it was about five degrees outside, with blizzard-like conditions. The truck that was supposed to deliver our furniture was snowbound back in Ohio and wouldn't arrive for a week and a half. We'd already bought a house, but it was still being renovated, so we'd made plans to stay with our friend Alice Koutsoumpas, who was originally from Terre Haute and whose son, Tom, had worked on my father's staff and been a good friend of mine since I was thirteen. As soon as we arrived at their house, I proceeded to lock my keys in the car with the engine running. I didn't have a spare, and the guy from the AAA Auto Club was stumped by the car's anti-theft protection system. Finally, after what was a very embarrassing half hour for me, he managed to open the door—an inauspicious start to say the least.

Our house was ready about ten days later, and we moved in on the day I was sworn in to office. We live in Spring Valley, near

American University. Today, it's a neighborhood in transition. Most of the homes were built in the 1940s, and many of the original owners still live there, but we're seeing more young families with children moving into the area. Our next-door neighbors, for instance, have a two-year-old. There are also a few other congressmen in the area: Senator Jeff Bingaman, a Democrat from New Mexico, lives six blocks away, and Senator Dianne Feinstein, a Democrat from California, recently bought a place not too far from ours.

When my father began his career as a senator in 1962, our family lived in the suburb of McLean, Virginia, but Susan and I wanted to live within the District so that I wouldn't have a long commute that would cut into my time with her and the boys. I knew I'd have to work late, and I wanted to be sure I'd be home as often as possible to tuck the boys into bed. From the house, it takes me about ten minutes to get to the boys' school and half an hour to get to Capitol Hill, which isn't bad. In Washington, a much longer commute isn't uncommon.

Because the cost of land in Washington is so high, the typical lot size is much smaller than what we were used to in Indiana, but our modest yard is fine by us. We're in a nice area with plenty of big trees, which was one of the things we liked so much about Meridian-Kessler—the shade in the summer, the beautiful leaves in the fall. Nick and Beau like the house, too. When we lived in the governor's residence and on Washington Boulevard, they shared a room, but now, they have separate rooms connected by a common bathroom. Growing up with two sisters, Susan never had a room of her own and always wanted one, so it was important to her that Nick and Beau each have his own space.

What seemed like a perfect house turned out to have a hidden flaw, though. In April 2001, an electrical malfunction started a fire in our attic. I'd just put the boys to sleep and Susan and I were packing for a trip when the lights went off in our bathroom. We thought it was just a fuse, but two or three minutes later the smoke detector upstairs went off. Fortunately, Susan had just changed the batteries in all of our smoke detectors. We got the boys out of the house immediately, and the fire trucks showed up within ten minutes.

We're lucky Susan and I were awake. Had the fire started in the middle of the night or when we were out of town and the kids home with only a sitter, it might have burned down the whole house with potentially tragic results. The blaze required ten engines, five ladder trucks, and a hundred firefighters. Though the fire was confined to the attic and roof, vast quantities of water used to extinguish it poured down into the lower floors. Though most of the interior of the house was gutted by smoke and water, our biggest loss occurred in the attic, where we stored a great many of our family memorabilia and keepsakes. During the ten months while the house was being renovated and repaired, we lived in a rented house nearby. Our friends were worried that the boys would be traumatized by the whole ordeal, but they weren't, because we weren't. Children take their emotional cues from their parents. Since none of us was hurt in the fire, Susan and I never treated it as a tragedy. Most material things can be replaced.

13

THE RESPONSIBLE FATHERHOOD ACT

*In Washington, we spend billions of dollars a year
dealing with the symptoms of the fatherhood crisis.*

BECOMING A U.S. Senator was quite a change for me, and not just
because I was moving from the state level to the federal level. My
father had been in the legislative branch throughout his career—
first in the state legislature, then eighteen years in the Senate—whereas my formative experience had been in the executive
branch. There are a host of differences between the two. If you want
to pass a bill in a legislature, you have to get a majority of votes. If
you're an executive, you speak for that branch of government. You
consult. You seek advice. You listen. But ultimately *you* decide. You
get to say, "Here's what I think, here's what we're going to do"—
and that's what I was accustomed to after ten years as governor and
secretary of state: running my office, making decisions, and implementing them. Now I was entering a very different working
environment, one in which decisions are made by a group, one with
different rhythms, rules, and customs.

I arrived in Washington at a time of unprecedented economic

prosperity in the United States. Nevertheless, many Americans felt our country was on the wrong track; they perceived a deterioration of values, one that was eroding the structure of families and fraying our social fabric. Of the many issues I wanted to address, father absence seemed the best place to start since it contributes to so many of our social problems and since nobody else in the Senate was making it a priority. Unfortunately, the day after I was sworn in, President Clinton's impeachment trial began—the first impeachment of a president since 1868. The trial consumed the first few months of the Senate session, a period during which virtually nothing else got done. My staff and I were already putting together The Responsible Fatherhood Act of 1999, my first bill as a United States senator, but we weren't able to introduce it until July 14.

In the months leading up to that day, I took the bill through the three-step process I use in crafting a piece of legislation. First, I establish the broad policy vision: What challenge do I want to address? In the case of The Responsible Fatherhood Act, the problem is that too many fathers are bringing children into the world and then walking away, leaving the mothers and society to pick up the pieces. That, in turn, is contributing to an array of other problems such as teen pregnancy, juvenile violence, incarceration, drug and alcohol abuse, educational underachievement, and economic underperformance—problems I'd been trying to address since I was first elected governor.

The second step is figuring out how to implement that policy vision: What laws will effectively address the problem? Specifically, how can we encourage men to be better, more responsible fathers? A politician may have the greatest policy vision in the world, but if he doesn't have a smart, well-constructed plan to accomplish his goals, his vision doesn't matter.

This second step is where one starts getting into specifics, really thinking the problem through. Those specifics eventually get translated by legislative aides into the actual language of the bill— a language that has only a vague approximation to English. I remember talking to a friend back home in Indiana shortly after I'd been elected to the Senate. "One thing I always regretted was that I never learned a foreign language," I said. "But now I have to, because English as we know it is rarely spoken in Washington."

The third step, for lack of a better term, is the art of politics. One must consider whether a policy is sustainable, because if the public won't support it, and if Congress won't pass it, it won't get implemented. Good intentions and eloquent speeches don't mean much if they don't lead somewhere. At the end of the day, a politician's work ought to be a *practical* undertaking: How do you actually get things accomplished that help people? Principled compromise is the key, and the challenge from a public-policy perspective is to push the envelope as far as you can in the direction that you believe is right, but not so far that you lose the consensus and end up getting *nothing* done.

In order to get a bill passed in the Senate, you usually need significant bipartisan support, so I cosponsored The Responsible Fatherhood Act with Pete Domenici, a highly respected senior Republican from New Mexico and a father of eight. Pete also brought a certain fiscal legitimacy to the bill. There's a healthy level of skepticism in the Senate whenever a member proposes a bill that provides money for a new government program—especially if that member is a Democrat. I'd worked hard to establish a reputation for fiscal responsibility when I was governor, but I was new to Washington, so my new colleagues didn't necessarily know about that aspect of my record.

I felt Pete's reputation for fiscal conservatism would send an important message to those senators who might be inclined to oppose the bill because of concerns about big government or runaway spending. The other senators know Pete is not some wild-eyed spender and that he wouldn't endorse an expenditure unless it was worthwhile. Also—as Joe Lieberman pointed out at the press conference when we introduced the bill—it's always good to have the Senate Budget Committee chairman as your lead cosponsor.

The Responsible Fatherhood Act built upon efforts I'd begun back in Indiana. I knew that we couldn't pass a law requiring men to be good fathers, and I certainly didn't feel that a national bureau of families would be the solution to the fatherhood crisis. But I did feel strongly that the federal government could work with existing efforts and bring badly needed resources to bolster the programs of state and local governments, community groups, and faith-based organizations with a track record of success. I also felt that the federal government should be seeking to remove barriers that kept families from staying together.

The aims of The Responsible Fatherhood Act were to spotlight the importance of families and marriage for child development; to strengthen fragile families; and to promote responsible fatherhood.

The bill had two sections. Title I sought to raise public awareness of the fatherhood crisis and to promote community involvement through a state-by-state media campaign, a state block-grant program, and the creation of a national clearinghouse to share best practices. A $25 million media-grant program would allow each state to air television ads that conveyed the importance of fatherhood (a grant program modeled on our efforts in Indiana, where we were so successful in leveraging dollars to cover the high expense of television advertising).

Title II sought to remove federal barriers to responsible fatherhood and two-parent, married families through increased job opportunities for unemployed fathers (via the Welfare to Work program), state incentives for programs that promote two-parent families and responsible fatherhood, and direct child-support payments to families. When a father pays child support to a mother who is on welfare, much of that money doesn't actually go to the mother and child, but rather to the state, as reimbursement for the welfare benefits being provided to the mother and child. Not surprisingly, when men find out their money is going to the state and not to their children, they're less inclined to make the payments. Under my bill, the job of reimbursing the states would fall to the federal government, not the father, and the majority of a father's child-support payments would go directly to the mother and child, thereby providing him with a stronger incentive to make payments.

It's important to note that getting men to pay their child support isn't just a financial issue. Studies show that men who pay child support are also more likely to take a greater interest in supporting their children emotionally as well.

In the months after we introduced the bill, I went around and talked to quite a few senators from both sides of the aisle, and I was able to bring several more cosponsors on board. (In addition to Pete Domenici, the original cosponsors included my Republican colleague from Indiana, Richard Lugar, plus well-regarded senators such as North Carolina Democrat John Edwards, Connecticut Democrat Joe Lieberman, Arkansas Democrat Blanche Lincoln, Ohio Republican George Voinovich, and others.)

I was also doing what I could to learn more about father absence and raise public awareness of the issue. One such opportunity came in October, when I met with participants of the Father Resource Program at Wishard Memorial Hospital in Indianapolis, a program that had received funds through the fatherhood grant program I started as governor. The Father Resource Program is designed to promote paternal prenatal care by targeting young, unwed, undereducated, underemployed fathers, mostly age seventeen to twenty-five. Research shows that the earlier a father takes an active interest in his kids, the better. If fathers are present at sonograms, for example, they're more likely to become involved in the lives of their children.

A Columbia University study showed that the presence of a father also positively impacts the mother's behavior during pregnancy, making her more likely to seek proper prenatal care and less likely to smoke, drink, or abuse drugs—especially if she's married to the father. Furthermore, the nature of the parents' relationship at the time of the baby's birth is a strong predictor of the father's future involvement in the child's life. If a father and mother aren't living together when their baby is born, the dad is less likely to take an active role in the child's life later on. The odds of the father being involved with the child are higher if the mother and father are living together, and higher still if they're married. The evidence is pretty clear: The presence of the father during pregnancy means healthier mothers, healthier babies, and healthier families. Men need to do their part.

The Father Resource Program has proven to be quite a success, moving many men into steady employment and into closer contact with their families. Participants have also shown themselves less likely to be incarcerated and more likely to attain their GEDs. On the day I was there, a dozen young fathers were sitting around the table. "Tell me how you got here," I said. "I want to hear your story." Most had become fathers when they were teens, most were high-school dropouts with few job skills, and many struggled with substance-abuse problems, but they were in this program because they wanted to get back on track. As one young father told me, "I never knew my dad, and I don't want my daughter to be saying the same thing about me someday."

Our wedding day, April 13, 1985. Our mothers had known each other since the 1968 Democratic convention, but Susan and I didn't meet until the summer of 1981.

In 1986, with Susan by my side, I ran for Indiana secretary of state—my first campaign.

Susan held our family Bible—and me—after I was sworn in as governor of Indiana in January 1989. At age thirty-three, I was the youngest governor in the country.

Left: Our proudest moment: in the hospital with Nick and Beau the day after they were born.

Below: Coming home with the boys from the hospital to the house at 4750 North Meridian Street in Indianapolis. They were the first children to live at that governor's residence.

Below: The boys' christening at Trinity Episcopal Church.

Indiana's First Family doubled in size with the arrival of the twins, and I wanted to share the good news everywhere I went.

It was an emotional time for my dad and me on Election Night 1988, when I became Indiana's first Democratic governor in twenty-four years. (*Indianapolis Star* photo by Rob Goebel)

Four days after my visit to Wishard, I was back in Washington to testify before the House Ways and Means Subcommittee on Human Resources in support of The Fathers Count Act of 1999, a bipartisan House bill. Though I was the first to introduce a fatherhood initiative in the Senate, several members of the House had been working on a similar measure. During my testimony, I discussed the considerable body of research showing the ill effects of fatherlessness, and I pointed to a study in the *Journal of Research in Crime and Delinquency* that found that the best predictor of violent crime and burglary in a community is not poverty, but the proportion of single-parent households. I also spoke about the success of programs such as the Father Resource Program and, in an effort to lay the groundwork for House-Senate cooperation on fatherhood legislation, drew attention to the many similarities between the Fathers Count Act and my own Responsible Fatherhood Act.

The House ended up passing its fatherhood bill that year, but The Responsible Fatherhood Act narrowly missed passage in the Senate. The Clinton Administration was supportive, though, and we negotiated to have the legislation included in one of the budget bills late in the session. Unfortunately, we ran out of time and weren't able to make it happen. I was disappointed, but it's an example of life in the Senate: You make a little progress one year, a little more the next year, and eventually you get something done. You just have to keep knocking at the door.

That's exactly what I did when the 2000 session began, lobbying for support among my colleagues and continuing to revise the bill to give it the best possible chance of passing. When we'd introduced The Responsible Fatherhood Act, we faced some initial skepticism from women's rights groups. When they hear "fatherhood," they sometimes think of organizations that celebrate men as the sole, rightful leaders of families. The women's rights groups had their antennae out to make sure that our bill included no hidden agenda to foster a patriarchal society, that it didn't insist on women reconnecting with abusive men and didn't reinforce gender stereotypes, such as the idea that women should be economically dependent upon men, or that men should be the only breadwinners in families.

As a strong supporter of equal rights for women (and as the son of the man who introduced the Equal Rights Amendment to Congress in 1970 and the spouse of an accomplished professional woman), I could appreciate their concerns. I think the fatherhood crisis is in many ways a women's rights issue, because what it comes down to is that too many men have been behaving irresponsibly, making women carry a disproportionate share of the parenting load.

Our fatherhood legislation was largely about addressing the adverse consequences women and children face when men act irresponsibly, and we certainly didn't want to *add* to those adverse consequences. We sat down with the concerned parties and explained what The Responsible Fatherhood Act was really about. We pointed out that some of the most successful fatherhood programs already incorporate a domestic-violence prevention component, teaching noncustodial parents to deal with their anger in a nonviolent and constructive manner.

We also made some important additions to the bill, including strong provisions to safeguard against spouse abuse. Those changes included clear statements that "responsible fatherhood" means being nonviolent and that any promotion of fatherhood must always recognize and promote the values of nonviolence. The changes require states to encourage fatherhood programs that receive funds under this legislation to coordinate with local domestic-violence programs. They also require states to ensure that these fatherhood programs have on hand state and local domestic-violence information and resource materials.

We also faced a certain degree of disinterest from some conservatives. The Heritage Foundation, which has a strong following in the Republican Party, emphasizes marriage as the answer to many of the problems we were seeking to address and would rather see us put together a pro-marriage bill than a responsible-fatherhood bill. But this shouldn't be an "either/or" situation. My view—and one that is strongly supported by research—is that marriage is the ideal family situation for successful child-rearing. The majority of children raised in single-parent homes turn out just fine, but study after study indicates that those children are more at risk than children raised in married households. Not coincidentally, marriage is also the single strongest predictor of a father's involvement in his child's life. But in the world as it exists today, with divorce rates running at nearly 50 percent, we have to be realistic and consider what's best for children when marriages don't work out. We should encourage marriage under the appropriate circumstances, but we can't coerce people into getting married, insist that women stay in abusive relationships or stigmatize single parents. What matters to me is that fathers do right by their kids regardless of family structure.

To make our bill more appealing to those on the right who otherwise might not take much interest in fatherhood issues, we added a marriage component, one that has since been embraced by President George W. Bush, too. That component provides grants to entities that promote responsible fatherhood, but it also allows those entities to use part of the money to promote marriage. Ultimately, the bill supports marriage as an ideal, but not as the only answer to the problem of father absence. It's all a matter of achieving the best outcome for kids. We're trying to identify the common ground between right and left, take the best from both.

Other conservatives were interested but skeptical. There tends to be a perception on the right that many Democrats are too permissive with regard to behavior that's harmful to society. Some conservatives weren't convinced that Democrats were really willing to support efforts to encourage successful marriages and to truly hold men accountable for their actions. In the end, however, I think we were able to overcome their skepticism.

Of course, we'll never completely satisfy all the interest groups who have been critical of the bill—nor would we want to. By their nature, interest groups tend to view the world from a purely ideological perspective, and they tend to take absolutist "all or nothing" positions: you're either with them 100 percent of the time or you're not—there's no room for principled compromise. Interest groups don't have to worry about whether their views can ever be enacted or actually help people. That's my job: determine what's right and devise a strategy for getting as much of it done as possible, forge a viable consensus, lend coherence to the cacophony of conflicting views.

Changing the bill to satisfy all interest groups would not only be impossible (since some have opposite and mutually exclusive goals), but it would also kill the bill's chances of garnering the necessary public and political support, and it would alter the bill so that it no longer embodied what I believe is the appropriate policy vision. In the end, I think we got the bill to the point where the interest groups didn't necessarily endorse it, but they didn't object, which is probably as good as you're going to do.

The fatherhood crisis got a welcome boost of publicity when Vice President Al Gore addressed the National Summit on Fatherhood on June 2, 2000. Gore has long been committed to the fatherhood movement, having spoken at the National Fatherhood Initiative's summit in 1994 and then again in 1998, when he chaired the National Summit Committee. I was doing my part to raise public awareness as well. On June 14, the Senate unanimously passed my resolution designating that Sunday, Father's Day, as "National Responsible Father's Day." The bill was only a symbolic gesture, but I believe symbols count for something, and Father's Day is an especially appropriate time to heighten awareness of the fatherhood crisis.

I was also having some success in garnering more support for The Responsible Fatherhood Act among my fellow senators. Daniel Patrick Moynihan of New York, the most senior Democrat on the Senate Finance Committee, which had jurisdiction over the bill, became its eighteenth cosponsor. Two other members of the Finance Committee had also signed on: Senator Paul Coverdell, a Republican from Georgia, and Senator James Jeffords, a Republican from Vermont who would make headlines the following May by leaving the GOP to become an independent, thus returning control of the Senate to the Democrats for the first time since 1994.

Perhaps the year's biggest breakthrough came in late July 2000, when the Senate convened its first-ever hearing on fatherhood initiatives. Getting a bill passed in Congress often involves an education process, but because there is so much going on and so little time, it's often hard to develop a consensus on an issue. Things either happen because they have to—because there's an emergency of some kind—or because a bill comes up for reauthorization and must be acted upon before it lapses into nonexistence.

Unfortunately, neither of those circumstances applies to our fatherhood legislation.

During my first year in the Senate, if I'd approached other members and said, "I want to discuss the fatherhood issue," most of them wouldn't have had the foggiest idea of what I was talking about. Many of them would have thought I was referring to a paternity suit. First you have to get an issue into the Congressional and public consciousness.

One of the most important ways of promoting a piece of legislation is by going to your colleagues who are on the committee of jurisdiction and saying, "This issue is important to me. Will you help me get the bill passed?" They'll usually say, "I don't know much about that issue, and we've got twenty other priorities to deal with right now. Why don't we have a hearing?" Basically, such hearings allow the committee members to make sure that you're not peddling a kooky idea. At the hearing, experts testify on the issue so the other senators (and, as importantly, their staffs) can learn what it's all about and hopefully become supporters of the bill. It's also a chance for the bill's author to gather feedback on how to improve the bill.

Once a bill has a hearing, it can then go to a committee vote, and from a committee vote, it can move onto the floor and, with hope, win approval from the Senate as a whole. Then it heads over to the House, where they go through a similar process. If the two chambers come up with different versions of the bill, it goes to a conference committee that reconciles the two versions and sends it back once again for passage by both bodies. Then, if everything works out, the bill goes to the president for his signature. Of course, there are a thousand complications that can occur along the way.

On the hot afternoon of July 25, 2000, the Senate's Social Security and Family Policy Subcommittee of the Finance Committee opened its hearing on fatherhood initiatives in room 215 of the Dirksen Senate Office Building. Among those testifying were my cosponsor, Pete Domenici, other members of Congress, and several fatherhood experts.

During my testimony, I spoke not only about the detrimental effect of father absence on children, but also about the fiscal importance of addressing this problem. In Washington, we spend billions of dollars a year dealing with the symptoms of the fatherhood crisis. The consequences of drug and alcohol abuse, for instance, cost the United States more than $110 billion per year; programs aimed at keeping kids in school cost the country $8 billion per year; poverty relief for families and children cost more than $105 billion in 1999; and teenage pregnancy and sexually transmitted diseases were estimated to cost more than $21 billion per year. I pointed to fatherhood initiatives as a way of embracing the old adage, "An ounce of prevention is worth a pound of cure."

Though the hearing stoked interest in the fatherhood crisis, it did not lead to any quick action on my bill, so when an opportunity arose to promote responsible fatherhood through another channel, I pursued it. That September, the House overwhelmingly voted in favor of Congresswoman Nancy Johnson's Child Support Distribution Act, legislation that included elements very similar to those found in my bill. Representative Johnson's bill was designed to pass child support more directly to families, regardless of whether they continued to receive public assistance. I joined forces with Senator Olympia Snowe, a Republican from Maine, in introducing Senate legislation that added key elements of my Responsible Fatherhood Act to The Child Support Distribution Act, including language to provide states with program grants for community-based fatherhood programs and a media-grant component designed to promote responsible fatherhood. My hope was that our new legislation would serve as a blueprint for compromise between the House and the Senate.

It was high time for Congress to get on the fatherhood bandwagon. By that time, President Clinton had praised the work of fatherhood programs in his State of the Union Address, and presidential candidates George W. Bush and Al Gore had both offered fatherhood proposals during their campaigns. In the end, though, Senator Snowe and I had no more luck than I'd had on my own with The Responsible Fatherhood Act.

The year 2000 was nevertheless a landmark year for fatherhood initiatives. I'd been lobbying hard to include fatherhood funds in the federal budget, and on December 19, I had the pleasure of announcing that in the fiscal year 2001, $3.5 million would go toward efforts to promote responsible fatherhood through media outreach and community-based programs. The funds were to be administered by the National Fatherhood Initiative and used for the same purpose proposed in Title I of The Responsible Fatherhood Act: to establish a national clearinghouse to share best practices. This was the first time the federal budget included funds for the promotion of responsible fatherhood.

I was especially pleased to see a portion of those funds go to Indiana. On June 15, 2001, I joined Roland Warren, president of the NFI, at the Children's Museum of Indianapolis to announce plans to launch the Indiana Fatherhood Initiative, making Indiana one of only four states in the country (along with Pennsylvania, Virginia, and Texas) to have a state-specific NFI program. When I'd held the Governor's Conference on Fatherhood five years earlier, one of my goals had been to make Indiana a model state in the fight against father absence. Now, with the establishment of the Indiana Fatherhood Initiative, Indiana was one step closer to that goal.

Today, the Indiana Fatherhood Initiative is headquartered in Indianapolis and addresses the problem of father absence using a three-pronged approach. First, the Initiative conducts public-awareness campaigns to underscore the importance of responsible fatherhood, including televised public-service announcements and donated print ads. Second, the Initiative sponsors local fatherhood forums across the state to help mobilize a response to the problem. Third, the program established an Indiana Fatherhood Resource Center to provide training, technical assistance, and consultation to community-based organizations throughout the state interested in implementing fatherhood outreach, support, or skill-building programs.

As of January 2003, five workshops had been held throughout Indiana to train fatherhood program personnel, and the IFI had provided technical assistance to more than ninety organizations. The IFI has also received $245,000 in donated media air-time, a remarkable $21.60 for every dollar spent by IFI.

14

THE RIGORS OF PUBLIC OFFICE

"Dad's famous, huh?"

MY PARENTS BENT over backwards to make sure my childhood was as normal as possible, and Susan and I are trying to do the same for Nick and Beau. It's very important to us that they enjoy the same experiences that other kids do. I don't want them to feel as if they're in a fishbowl, and I don't want what I do for a living to interfere with or unduly influence what they do with their own lives. They know that we represent Indiana in Washington, not the reverse, and they look forward to our trips home. They like to demonstrate their loyalty by cheering for and wearing the jerseys of Indiana college and professional sports teams.

I don't want them to think that their dad—or what he does for a living—is much different from anyone else. In that regard, and when it comes to my family's privacy, it's probably easier being a member of Congress than governor or mayor. The boys are able to lead somewhat anonymous lives in Washington. Nobody at the grocery store or the mall knows who they are; their classmates treat them the same as other children. However, if I were a mayor or still governor, things would be different. The boys would read about me

117

in the newspaper every day. They'd see more stories about me on TV. For better or worse, everyone would know who they are: "Oh, you're the governor's son!"

Fortunately, the press is pretty good about respecting the privacy of children. Susan and I have made public appearances with the boys—the Democratic National Convention in Chicago being perhaps the best-known—but we've been careful not to overdo it. The key, I think, is shielding them until they're old enough to make their own decisions about how public a life they want to lead.

At this point, I don't think Nick and Beau know a great deal about my job, and that's how I like it. I just want them to think of me as their father, period, which is how I thought of my own father. I always admired the fact that he never had a big ego or thought that being a senator made him better than anyone else. But I know the day is coming when they'll realize that I'm a public figure and begin to understand what that entails. At last year's Brickyard 400 in Indianapolis, after seeing a number of people walk up to chat with me, Beau turned to his mother and said, "Dad's famous, huh?"

In general, it seems the children of public figures fall into one of two categories: those who admire their parents and the work they do (and who often pursue the same kind of work), and those who are turned off by public life and reject it (perhaps because they feel that public life impinged upon their relationship with their parents). Obviously, I fall squarely in the first category. My father treated me in such a way that I never felt I had to compete with the world for his attention. I volunteered to work on his campaigns, and I feel fortunate to have fashioned a career in public service as he did.

I hope that one day my sons will have an appreciation for what I do for a living, which is basically to create more opportunities for more Americans and help them make the most of their God-given abilities. I hope they'll see the importance of giving something back in life. At the same time, if Nick or Beau came to me and said he was interested in running for public office, my first feeling would be one of concern. Politics can be a hard career choice, and political life today is much nastier than it should be. Rather than engaging in civil debate, some people in the public arena express themselves in rude, hurtful ways.

Over the years I've received a fair amount of hate mail—though some of it has been more comic than hateful. I remember Fred Glass, my chief of staff, coming into my office with a letter once during my days as governor. I had just been forced to cut the budget, including a much deserved raise for state employees, because of an economic downturn, and a lot of people were angry. Down at the statehouse, somebody was putting up pictures over the urinals that showed mug shots of a squirrel—front and side views—with my name at the bottom.

"Governor," Fred said, "I thought you might want to see a complimentary letter you received."

"Sure," I said. "I can always use that."

"Dear Governor," the letter began, "you must have balls the size of cannonballs"—Fred's tongue-in-cheek idea of a compliment. The letter writer then proceeded to explain why he was dissatisfied with me. "I'll never vote for you for anything," he concluded. "If Jack the Ripper were your opponent, I still wouldn't vote for you. At least he gave it to his victims face to face, not in the back."

A year and a half later, after I was reelected, the same guy sent me another unsigned letter, but I recognized the handwriting. "Dear Governor Bayh," he began, "Congratulations on getting reelected. You may be able to fool most of the people in the state, but you can't fool me. I know what you're going to be doing to us for the next four years. I only ask that you keep it safe. Please use the enclosed." Inside the envelope was a condom.

Other times, the criticism has been much sharper. I've been maligned as self-centered, corrupt, a spendthrift, being indifferent to the suffering of the poor, possessing alien values, and much more. I've been called everything from a murderer, to a felon, to an imbecile; there have been times when people have refused to shake my hand. And I've been very fortunate, never having been subjected to the type of vitriol that my father and many others have.

Even though it's all part of the job, and every official from George Washington on has survived it, I don't like to think about my sons being subjected to public life's coarser side. I want them to work hard and make a contribution to the world, but if they choose to do so through politics, it should be because it's what they want to do, not because it's what their father did.

From the outside, holding political office can seem pretty glamorous, and there's no doubt the job offers a certain degree of ego gratification—the applause, the power, the media attention—but in my experience, the appeal of all that wears off pretty quickly. The only reason to run for public office—the *only* reason—is because there's something that you want to accomplish that you think is good for your city or state or country. If you seek public office for any other reason, I guarantee that at the end of the day, you won't be happy.

For kids, there's a mystique about what it is we parents do all day, so even though the boys don't fully understand my job, visiting Dad's office is still a big deal to them. When I was governor, Susan would often bring them to the state capitol where they'd crawl across my desk like two little tanks, scattering pens and papers in their wake. They made their first trip to Capitol Hill for my swearing-in ceremony on the floor of the Senate. Susan insisted we buy them little blue blazers for the occasion—the only time they've worn them—and we've got some cute pictures of them all dressed up, neckties askew. I don't think the ceremony was all that memorable for them, but they had a great time riding the underground tram that connects the Senate office buildings to the Capitol.

These days, the boys visit me at work about once a month or so. When I have to work late, Susan will sometimes pick up a pizza and the three of them will come to my office for dinner, or we'll all go over to the Capitol to eat at the Senate Restaurant. The boys also come to my various staff and holiday parties. A couple of years ago at the Christmas party, Beau started to get a little bored, so we stepped out into the hallway to toss a football. My office is in the Russell Senate Office Building, a Beaux Arts structure with marble staircases, a domed rotunda, and a grand Caucus Room which has hosted hearings on everything from the sinking of the *Titanic* in 1912 to Watergate in 1974. As Beau and I played catch beneath the hallway's soaring ceiling, our aim wasn't the best, and we occasionally hit the walls and even the door across the hall from mine—the door to the office of Senator Hillary Rodham Clinton. Next thing we knew, an alarmed Secret Service agent stepped into the hallway to assess the situation. When the agent got a look at us, he had a good laugh and went back inside. We weren't exactly a security threat.

The Senate has become a much more kid-friendly place in the last three or four years. The House is a much bigger body than the Senate, and its members tend to be younger, so there have always been a fair number of Representatives with kids, but this traditionally has not been the case in the Senate. Now, however, several of us have young children, including John Edwards from North Carolina and Peter Fitzgerald from Illinois. Blanche Lincoln, from Arkansas, has twin boys, Reece and Bennett, who are only a few months younger than Beau and Nick. Blanche and I were in the same freshman Senate class. She first came to Congress as a member of the House in 1992, but when she learned she was expecting in 1996—and that it was a high-risk pregnancy—she put her health and her kids first, deciding not to seek reelection. A year later, after her twins were born, she ran for the Senate and won. These days, when we have Senate retreats, the organizers try to pick places that are family- and kid-oriented, whereas a few years ago, I don't think they even gave children much of a thought.

15
TIME WITH MY SONS

Whatever we play, the one unspoken rule is Dad always loses.

PARENTS LOVE TO shake their heads and remark to other parents about how fast kids grow up, but even if you've heard this refrain a million times (as most of us have) it's still a source of wonder to watch your own children make the seemingly quick transition from helpless infants to sharp-minded little people with ideas and opinions of their own. Raising Nick and Beau has been great from the start—there's nothing like the moment when I first held them at the hospital—but for me, it's an experience that keeps getting better. And it's made me a better person, teaching me patience and the unconditional nature of love. For the first two-and-a-half or three years, being a parent sometimes felt like a one-way street—there wasn't a lot of interaction. Now that the boys are a little older, I feel like I'm a lot more involved with them because we can do things together, go places, carry on a conversation. Just being able to sit down as a family and eat a meal is a great blessing. Until they were three or four, they'd be knocking stuff over as we tried to feed them, crying and carrying on, and then they'd finish and want to leave the table—usually before Mom and Dad even took a bite.

Now they're old enough that we can all sit down for dinner together.

Our family always prays before we eat, and the boys have assumed the responsibility of saying grace. One of their favorites is the Johnny Appleseed Prayer, which they learned at school: "The Lord is good to me / and so I thank the Lord / for giving me the things I need / the sun, the rain, and the apple seed / the Lord is good to me." We all hold hands, the boys sing the prayer, and then they bless the people they care about.

But life with Nick and Beau isn't always so harmonious. They've been together since they were in the womb, so, not surprisingly, they know how to push each other's hot buttons. I'd say 90 percent of the time, they get along great, but the other 10 percent of the time, they have to work out their differences. These days Beau is the bigger of the two, but that doesn't stop Nick from needling him. I'm often reminded of something my mother's aunt, Lillian Tharp, once said. Susan had asked Auntie what I was like as a young boy. "Evan was a normal boy," Auntie said. *"A real stinker."* I'd say the same about Nick and Beau: they're fundamentally good boys, never malicious—which is something I've very proud of—but they can certainly be mischievous.

In the fall of 2002, the boys started first grade at Beauvoir. But before they were admitted to prekindergarten there, they had to take aptitude tests and go in for an interview. I remember scoffing at the admissions process. "They're four years old!" I said to Susan. "We'll be lucky if they don't hide under the chair." Nevertheless, they made it through the test and the interview, thanks largely to their mother, who successfully employed both threats and bribes: "If you behave during this interview, we'll go to McDonalds—and if you don't, there will be big trouble." The test results said Beau would be more verbally inclined, and Nick would be more mathematically inclined. Sure enough, that's exactly how they've turned out—so far.

Nick is the numbers guy in our family, a trait he probably gets from Susan's father, an engineer. He loves computers, playing chess, and reading the sports page. When he wakes up in the morning, the first words out of his mouth are, "Dad, who won?" Then he'll ask me the score of the Pacers game, who led the team in rebounds, who notched a double-double. Nick tends to be a little more tolerant than Beau, but he gets particularly upset when Beau doesn't play by the rules. Nick also likes to show off his mathematical ability by tormenting his brother with multiplication and division questions, but we try to nip such behavior in the bud. We tell them both that bragging is not allowed.

Beau is more creatively inclined than Nick. Susan's side of the family is probably responsible for that trait, too: she's quite handy, and her sister is a professional artist. Beau likes to draw and color, has a large vocabulary, is a gifted reader, and is gregarious. But he likes sports, too. At this point, he's actually stronger, faster, and bigger than his brother—one of the biggest boys in his grade—though Nick, who has larger feet, might yet end up bigger. Beau also tends to be more impatient than his brother, which is something that both he and his dad need to work on.

I've personally given tours of the Capitol to both of the boy's classes, but I have at least as much fun visiting them at school as they have coming to see me at work. On Parents Day last year, Susan and I took turns going between the boys' classes so we'd each get to spend time with both of them. When I was in Beau's class, they had "circle time," which is when the teacher goes around the room and asks each of the children to comment on what he or she likes best about the class. The teacher went in alphabetical order, so Beau was near the beginning. He said that what he liked best were his friends. Then, after all the kids had a turn, the teacher said, "Do any of the parents have anything they'd like to say?" Beau proceeded to volunteer me by grabbing my arm and raising my hand, at which point I had to think of something to say. I told them that I was impressed by how polite they were, and that they did a much better job than my colleagues in Congress at not interrupting one another.

When it was time to switch, I went over to Nick's class. He's a bit more on the shy side than Beau—you could tell as soon as he saw me come into the room. I kept a low profile so I wouldn't embarrass him. That semester, the kids were taking turns being the Person of the Day, who was responsible for going over the daily schedule and helping the teacher. Nick had been Person of the Day earlier in the week, and I remember wishing I'd been there to see that, how proud he must have been in his quiet way.

During the week, I work long hours, but I make it a point to spend as many weekends with Nick and Beau as I can. Sundays we try to go church as often as we can, usually St. Columba's Episcopal, although we haven't yet found a church in Washington where we feel the sense of closeness we enjoyed so much at Trinity Episcopal in Indianapolis.

Saturdays, though, are for playing. My perfect Saturday starts with an early morning run. After a quick shower, I put on some jeans and an old ball cap, round up the boys, and we head for the park. After we play for a couple hours, we usually grab lunch at a deli or fast-food place (Nick is testing whether it's possible to grow to adolescence without ingesting a green vegetable), then go out and play some more until late afternoon.

If it's rainy, Susan and I will sometimes take the boys to the movies, but mostly I like getting outdoors, and they do, too. We usually play sports—kicking the soccer ball, throwing football, shooting baskets. Our local park has a six-foot basketball goal, an eight-foot goal, and a ten-foot goal, so the boys can practice on all three. They also like the swing set at the playground, and we have a game of chase that we play, a glorified version of tag. We used to wrestle, but they're getting too big for that—if they gang up on me, I'm in trouble. Whatever we play, the one unspoken rule is that Dad always loses. This generally leads to the happiest outcome—as long as I put up a credible fight.

In the summer, Susan and I sometimes take the boys for bike rides, but swimming is their favorite hot-weather activity. It's good exercise, and it tires them out so they sleep better at night. For family vacations, we like to go to the beach—especially the Florida coast or the islands off New England—and, of course, back home to Indiana. In the winter, we usually go skiing at Beaver Creek in Colorado. The boys have been there two or three times, and they enjoy it. They're also into hockey, which I never played because it wasn't a popular sport in Indiana when I was growing up. Last winter, after I went to a couple of their hockey practices, the boys finally talked me into putting on a pair of ice skates. I was forty-six at the time, and I hadn't skated in forty years. I'm happy to report I didn't hurt anybody else or myself, but that didn't diminish the boys' glee. Nick kept zipping up to me and asking with eager anticipation, "Dad, did you fall yet?"

The boys and I also watch a lot of sports together. We catch the Pacers and Colts, Indiana, Purdue, and Notre Dame whenever they're on TV, and last year we went to see them in person at the MCI Center when they were in Washington to play the Wizards. I've also taken them to a Redskins game, a Capitals hockey game, and to a few local high school basketball games. High-school hoops is great entertainment, without the expense or hassles of a pro game, and even though the boys don't know the teams or the players, they're still impressed. "Wow," they say. "Those are the *big* boys."

Taking them to see the Redskins was quite an experience. It was late 2001, and the team had instituted new security measures in the wake of September 11. The line to get into the stadium was hundreds of people deep, it was freezing outside, and the crowd was rowdy. When one guy whipped off his shirt and waved it over his head, showing off a torso covered in tattoos, I began to get a little nervous standing there with three six-year-olds (the boys had brought along a friend). A few minutes later, a drunk got belligerent and the police had to wade into the crowd and subdue him. The guy practically landed in the boys' laps. That's when they started wondering if we were all going to get arrested. I assured them no, that was not the case. Of course, the next day at school, they weren't telling their friends they went to see a football game; they were telling them that their dad had taken them to see a man get arrested.

The boys and I also spend a good deal of time reading together. I usually read the sports page with them before they go off to school in the morning, and then at night I read with them in bed. Susan and I felt it was important to begin reading to them at a very early age. We started out with books such as *The Big Red Barn*, *Goodnight Moon*, and *The Very Bad Bunny*, and eventually graduated to Dr. Seuss. These days, I mostly help them read to *me*.

Putting the boys to bed is one of my favorite things to do. Over the years, we've developed a nightly routine where I sing songs to them; they call it "the full repertoire": "America the Beautiful," hymns from church, the IU fight song, whatever I know the words to. I've even made up a little lullaby for them: "Close your eyes, go to sleep / Time to rest now, my darlings / Know we love you very much / And we always will / Close your eyes now, and rest / May your slumber be blessed / Close your eyes now, and rest / Beau and Nick are the best." I also tell them a story each night. Sometimes I put Beau and Nick in the stories, and sometimes I draw the stories from history. It's fun trying to explain something like the Trojan War in such a way that it's interesting to six-year-olds. After we're done with the songs and stories, we say our prayers and I tuck them in. I like them knowing that I'm there for them when they go to sleep.

16
KEEPING IN TOUCH WITH HOME

*Now that the boys are in Washington much of the
time, it's very important to me that they maintain a
strong sense of their Hoosier roots.*

I BELIEVE IT'S important to always keep in mind where you're from
and who you represent, and for me that's Indiana. Washington is an
interesting town, and a public official can get good things accomplished there, but it's not the real world, and it certainly isn't home.
After working in Washington for a few years, I can see how politicians get cut off from the rest of the country. They're constantly
bombarded by special interests, a bombardment that can distort
one's perception of what really matters to the American public. As
governor, I used to enjoy working with the private sector to attract
new investment, create new jobs, help businesses grow, and raise the
standard of living for working people. A lot of people here in
Washington don't think about those things often enough.

I've made a few good friends since arriving on Capitol Hill, but
if the title "Senator" didn't come before my name, I think a lot of
people in Washington might not care so much about me. I
understand that a certain level of artificiality comes with the job,

but it nevertheless speaks to the nature of the town. My long-standing friends tend to be in Indiana, and every time I go home, I'm reminded of what a great place it is. I don't mean to sound like a cheerleader for the local tourism board, but people in Indiana tend to be more forthright, more open, more friendly. They're also by and large hardworking people with solid values. By no means do I think Hoosiers are perfect, but I do believe that Indiana is a far better microcosm of our country than is Washington.

Now that the boys are in Washington much of the time, it's very important to me that they maintain a strong sense of their Hoosier roots. My heart sang recently when I asked Beau what his favorite vacation was, and he replied, "Going home to Indiana."

I wish they'd had a chance to spend time on our family farm in Shirkieville, but my father had to sell the house and part of the land in order to pay for law school, and he sold the rest a few years ago to the same people who'd bought the first parcel. Fortunately, the new owners are longtime neighbors, and they've invited us to bring the boys around any time, which I'm looking forward to doing.

We've made a point of taking them to the Indiana State Fair every year. The fair director and his wife, Bill and Jane Stinson, are good friends, and we enjoy seeing the sights with them and their daughters, who are about our boys' age. Naturally they love the rides, but I like to show them the livestock, giving them a sense of their agricultural heritage. Our deal is that we always start with the animals, and then as soon as the boys can talk me into it, we head over to the midway, where the rides are. Eating is also a major part of our state fair experience. Corn on the cob dripping with butter, elephant ears, pork, beef, chicken, milk shakes from the Dairy Bar—we try it all.

Nick and Beau would like to spend more time in Indiana, but I'm not always able to bring them along when I come home. They've got school; plane tickets are expensive; and when I'm traveling in Indiana, my schedule is usually even more packed than when I'm in Washington. On average, I'm in Indiana at least once every ten days or so—less when the Senate is in session, but six or seven days at a time when we're out of session. Susan and I no longer own the house on Washington Boulevard, but we bought a two-bedroom condominium near Eighty-sixth Street on Indianapolis' Northside. We bring the boys back home for at least a full week or two every August, and then periodically throughout the rest of the year.

As they get older, I hope they'll spend more time in Indiana. I'm looking forward to taking them to their first Pacers and Colts games, and to visiting the Indiana Basketball Hall of Fame in New Castle to see the display mentioning their great-grandfather. I'd like to take them to Bloomington for a game at Assembly Hall, and also to Purdue, where my father took me more than thirty-five years ago to see the first basketball game ever played in Mackey Arena. I'd like them to experience a crisp autumn afternoon of Notre Dame football, and I also wouldn't mind seeing the boys attend Culver Military Academy for a few summers, as I did. I think they'd enjoy it, the discipline would be good for them, and I know Susan would appreciate (as my mother did) her sons learning the fine art of making their beds, folding their clothes, and generally keeping their things neat. I only hope the A&W Root Beer stand in Plymouth is still there.

Like good Hoosier boys, they're also keenly interested in basketball. I remember when I first played ball with Nick, the two of us lying on our backs in the governor's residence, me tossing a fuzzy ball into the air. He was fascinated by it even then, and to this day, he loves shooting basketball. He'd shoot all day if we let him—three-pointers, lay-ups, turnaround jumpers—and he does quite well for a seven-year-old. I wish I could say he got it from me. Beau loves to drive to the basket and rebound. Being the tallest boy in his grade, he's "Mr. Inside" to his brother's "Mr. Outside." The boys often play ball with kids who are a year or two older. I remember last spring, when Nick and Beau were still in kindergarten, one of the first graders on the playground asked how they got to be so good at basketball.

Beau replied, "We're from Indiana."

I liked that. And if my experience is any indication, Nick and Beau may actually become more devoted ambassadors of Indiana and all things Hoosier for having lived outside the state. We're proud of where we're from and, without being boastful, aren't shy about letting people know.

17
VALUES

Children can tell when you're serious about
something, and it makes an impact on them.

MY PARENTS USED to tell me, "If we could have ordered a child out of the Sears & Roebuck catalog, we would have picked you." To this day I am awed and humbled to think how much of herself my mother poured into me. She was first diagnosed with cancer when I was fifteen, and I've come to see that a big part of what kept her going during her fight to live was her devotion to me. She wanted to see me through my childhood and ensure that I became a well-rounded person, ready to face adulthood. It was only after she'd done that—after I'd graduated from high school and college and begun my first year of law school—that she passed away.

I'm now forty-seven, only a year older than my mother was when she died, and her death continues to be a strong reminder that I can never take my children, or life, for granted, not even for a second. It's particularly important to me that I be here for Nick and Beau now, during their formative years, because there's no guarantee I'll have a chance to make up for lost time down the road.

There's a lot of talk about "family values" in Washington, and exactly what the term means depends upon who's doing the talking. Whatever the definition, I believe it is important that a public official's public values and personal values are consistent. In our house, loving our children unconditionally is the most important family value. Of course, character values such as honesty, kindness, fairness, and integrity are also very important to Susan and me. We want to instill in our boys a strong sense of right and wrong; we want them to learn to control their frustration or anger and develop self-discipline; we want them to have respect for others. We don't allow them to make fun of people using even the most innocent words, because we don't want them to fall into the habit of saying unkind things about others. Nevertheless, seven-year-olds will inevitably call each other names and test the boundaries of acceptable behavior. I remember one day last year when Beau climbed onto my lap after work.

"Dad, are you going to tell us about the 'F' word?"

"What?" I said. "I never want to hear you mention that again."

"I didn't say the word, I just want to know if *you* know the 'F' word."

I told him that if I ever heard him use that word, I'd wash his mouth out with soap.

Then Nick chimed in. "Well, what about the 'S' word?"

"That too!" I said.

It wasn't until later that Susan explained to me that they thought the "F" word was "fat" and the "S" word was "stupid." What a relief.

Another day, Beau came home singing a Britney Spears song. I could only hope that he hadn't seen the video. In one popular movie we watched together—a movie marketed explicitly to children— one of the lead characters says, "You're full of s---." Nick turned to me and, not knowing what he was saying, repeated the line. I was shocked—and angry. I'm not a prude, but I don't think that suggestive materials or obscenities are appropriate for a seven-year-old.

Of course, that's an occupational hazard of parenthood these days: navigating the culture we live in, deciding what your child is and isn't ready for. Susan and I spend a lot of time trying to compensate for our children's exposure to the coarseness of life and explaining that just because something is on TV or another child does it, that doesn't make it right or acceptable (just as my mother taught me so many years ago that it's not acceptable to put your feet up on the table—even if LBJ himself did it).

Trying to instill good values in my children is at least as challenging as any of the responsibilities I face as a senator. How do you explain to a seven-year-old, for instance, that a person's true worth has nothing to do with money or race or religion? How do you actually instill in your kids an appreciation for the importance of respecting other people? Sometimes when Nick and Beau behave in unacceptable ways, I tell myself, "I'm going to be reasonable. We'll talk things out rationally," but reasoning with seven-year-olds can be an exercise in futility. Susan and I struggle with these challenges just like all the other parents we know. In the end, there is no magic wand. We just try to teach our boys the old-fashioned way: by example and through repetition, day after day. Just as good public servants live by the values they publicly advocate, good parents live by the values they seek to instill in their children. But walking the walk isn't enough. You also have to talk to your kids, letting them know that your convictions are strong. Children can tell when you're serious about something, and it makes an impact on them.

My father was sometimes one of only two or three parents at

my Little League games, but even though he made every effort to be involved in my life, his job often kept him away from home. His campaigns required a great deal of travel, and when he wasn't on the campaign trail, he still had to make frequent trips back to Indiana to stay in touch with his constituents. My mother once said she wished he were the senator from Alaska—a state too far away for him to be making such weekend trips.

Now that I'm the one making those trips, I know how my father must have felt trying to juggle his job and his home life. In order to spend more time with Susan and the boys, I've learned to concentrate my travel so that I'm home in Indiana for longer periods of time, rather than traveling every few days. Susan has to travel for her work, too, so we always try to make sure that at least one of us is home when the boys go to bed and when they wake in the morning. (We're fortunate to live close to Susan's father and Jane Sinnenberg, who help with the boys on the rare occasions when both Susan and I are gone.) I've also learned to be selfish with my time when I'm in Washington. The nation's capital has a very active social life, and I could attend a function every night of the week, but being with my family is a higher priority, and I like being a homebody when I can and saying "no" to all except the most important invitations.

Still, there are some events I can't miss, some trips I can't cut short, some late nights I can't avoid. All too often after putting the kids to bed I'll work until midnight. Like most parents in America, I wish I got more sleep, but that's the price I pay for having a job that I love and that I take very seriously. I'm proud of the fact that during my first three years I didn't miss a single vote in the Senate, though my duties as a dad have made for some close calls.

I remember one in particular. Two years ago, Beau, who has a low, strong voice, landed a speaking role in a performance at school.

Susan was out of town, so it was doubly important that I attend. That afternoon, I had one of my aides drive me over so that I could get some work done on the way. Just as we arrived at the school, my cell phone rang. It was another one of my aides telling me that the majority leader had just called a vote. If I was going to make it, I'd have to hustle back to Capitol Hill immediately.

I don't even remember what we were voting on, except that it was fairly inconsequential, a procedural matter. The vote itself wasn't the issue. The leader had called it on the spur of the moment to intentionally inconvenience members, thereby sending a message that he was unhappy about what was going on in the Senate at that time. It's a tactic designed to spur action and is not the sole province of Republicans; Democrats employ the same measures. Such are the strange, mysterious workings of the United States Congress—not dissimilar I sometimes think from the workings of my children's classes. An understanding of human psychology and group dynamics are important to grasping the behavior of legislative bodies.

Getting back to Capitol Hill in time for the vote wasn't going to be easy. In Washington, one is very much at the mercy of traffic. Part of the problem is the way the city is built. For aesthetic reasons, the height of commercial buildings is restricted to keep them from dwarfing the public buildings and monuments; as a result, there are no skyscrapers in Washington. Since developers aren't able to build up, they build out, and the suburban sprawl goes on for miles. The worst rush-hour traffic in Indianapolis doesn't compare to a normal day in D.C. And heaven help you if the weather is bad.

The trip from the National Cathedral to the Capitol would ordinarily take twenty minutes, but it happened to be 5 P.M. I was looking at a thirty-five-minute ride. Oddly enough, there's a law on the books in Washington to help Congressmen in such situations. It states that if a vote is in progress, a Congressman can disregard traffic regulations in order to reach the Capitol on time. However, my aide and I decided it would be too dangerous to speed through red lights in heavy traffic, so we got back as fast as we could without invoking that law. Fortunately, Senator Tom Daschle, the minority leader, stalled the proceedings, and when I arrived at the Capitol, I literally ran into the Senate and was able to cast my vote in time. Not that I affected the outcome—the tally was a hundred-to-nothing.

"Where were you?" a colleague asked me.

I told them I was at a performance at the boys' school.

"And you came back for this? You missed the performance for this?" They looked at me like I was crazy. "For God's sake, next time, don't do it."

But the day had a happy ending, after all. As soon as I voted, I hopped back into the car and made it to the National Cathedral in time to see Beau's big moment and the conclusion of the performance.

Discipline is another value that Susan and I hold dear. We quickly learned that if we didn't lay down the law, the boys would walk all over us, but if we did, they'd complain but usually respect it. We used to send them to their rooms when they misbehaved, but the effectiveness of that has worn off—they've learned to amuse themselves in their rooms. Withholding dessert remains a good enforcement tool, but these days the most effective means of punishment is to deny them television, the use of the computer, or—heaven forbid—their Game Boy (which has already been banished in our household on weekdays). I can't say the boys have ever really been spanked, but on those very rare occasions when they actually physically endanger themselves, stronger measures can be required. They could get killed running into the street or playing with a bottle of Drain-O, and if a gentle swat on the behind effectively reinforces that message, I think it's worth it.

But discipline isn't just about punishment. We believe that good behavior starts with a strong relationship between parent and child, one of mutual respect. When I was growing up, I didn't like being grounded or having to surrender the car keys, but my parents' approval was the most important thing to me: I tried to behave because I didn't want to disappoint them. I felt bad when I let them down. The same is true for our boys, and it's a reciprocal feeling. I hope that my boys want my respect and approval, but I hope I have theirs as well.

Though children will complain about discipline now and then, I believe that deep down, they actually want it. I don't think kids who live in overly permissive homes are as happy as children who live in well-structured environments. On some basic level, kids need the security of knowing they have to meet certain standards of behavior. Growing up in a home without rules and boundaries is (to borrow Robert Frost's description of free-verse poetry) akin to playing tennis without a net.

Susan and I are lucky in that we see eye to eye on most parenting issues. The same was true of my parents, though as a child, I thought my mother was much stricter than my father. I understand now that it was just a matter of her being at home and having to dole out more discipline than my father did, but back then, I associated him with all the fun activities, such as playing sports and going on vacation. I'm afraid the same is probably true for my boys. When I get home from work, I don't want to spend that precious time disciplining them; I naturally prefer that we do enjoyable things if we can. Somebody has to be the heavy, though; somebody has to make sure they learn to follow rules, have decent manners, and respect authority. The bulk of the job inevitably falls to Susan, since she is with them more. Susan says she always thought she'd be a much nicer parent (and in truth she's one of the most loving parents I know), but she can be quite tough when need be, especially concerning how Nick and Beau treat one another and other children.

I always back her up but usually am not as demanding as Susan—except when they're impolite to their mother. I have zero tolerance for that. Boys learn a lot about how to treat women from their father's behavior, especially toward their mother. I want Nick and Beau to know that their mother is loved and respected and, in our house, is the first among equals. And even though the boys might think of me as the fun parent, it's Susan they want when the chips are down. In the middle of the night, when they've got a headache or an upset stomach, they'll walk all the way around my side of the bed to get to hers.

Susan and I are occasionally asked if we plan to have more children. I'd love to have more, though I think Susan has a few reservations, considering neither of us is getting any younger, and with each passing year, a pregnancy could pose additional health risks for the baby. In terms of how the boys would feel about a new sibling, I suspect Beau wouldn't mind; he's very caring for younger children, particularly babies. I'm not so sure about Nick. He loves our family the way it is and likes having his time with Mom and Dad. I suspect he might be a little more reluctant to share us with a new brother or sister, though I'm sure in the fullness of time he'd get used to it. At any rate, our philosophy at this point is to let nature take its course. We're not going to try for more kids. We're blessed to have our two boys and couldn't be happier; if there's a surprise in store at some point, that would just be a cherry on top of the sundae.

18

POLITICAL ISSUES

I knew that if the president made fatherhood a
priority, Congress and the public would, too.

As SOON AS the Florida recount was completed and Al Gore ceded
the presidential election to George W. Bush on December 13, 2000,
speculation started about the next election. Who would run for the
Democrats in 2004? A number of people asked me if I'd give it some
thought, and I did, because I knew that as president of the United
States, I'd be in the best possible position to advance the policies that
I believe are good for Hoosiers and Americans. On the other hand,
I had my family to think about. What impact would a presidential
campaign have on Susan and the boys? I'd watched my father wrestle
with that question twice. As I mentioned earlier, he ended up
dropping out of the 1972 presidential race because my mother developed breast cancer, and family considerations contributed to his
delayed entry into the 1976 presidential race.

In the summer of 2000, I found myself weighing career against
family when there was talk that Al Gore might ask me to be his vice-
presidential running mate. He'd interviewed me for the post, and I

was among his four finalists, along with Senators John Edwards, John Kerry, and Joe Lieberman, whom Gore picked on August 8. Had the vice president asked me to join his ticket, I would have said yes—a decision Susan and I discussed at length. Since vice-presidential candidates aren't chosen until the party conventions in late summer of the election year, a vice president's campaign is a relatively short affair, requiring prolonged absence from family for only two or three months.

Running for president in 2004 would have required a much more substantial commitment, though. I know it's possible to simultaneously be a good governor and a good father, and I know it's possible to be an effective United States senator and a good father, but I wasn't convinced that it was possible to run for president and be a good father to two children as young as Nick and Beau.

Being a candidate for president is an all-consuming job. As a senator, I'm already away from home more than the average parent, but running for president doesn't mean being gone a lot; it means being gone *all* the time. If I had a free evening, I wouldn't be home for dinner; I'd be in New York or Boston. If I had a weekend off, I wouldn't be playing ball with the boys; I'd be in Iowa or New Hampshire. And if I had a free week, I wouldn't be going on a family vacation; I'd be in California and several other states. These days, a run for the presidency extends well beyond the election year, effectively consuming the better part of three to four years. If I were going to give it my full effort—which is the only way I'd do it—I'd essentially have to reconcile myself to being an absentee parent not for a period of weeks or months, but for a period of years.

The boys were five years old at the time, and as a parent, I was keenly aware of the importance of those early formative years. You only get one bite at the apple. Had my boys been older, as I was when my father first ran for president, I might have felt differently.

Susan said she'd support my decision, whether I chose to run or not. We talked about it for hours. Her one concern was that if I didn't run, I might always regret it. She didn't want me to feel as if she and the children were in some way keeping me from reaching the pinnacle of my life's work. She didn't want me to be kicking myself when I'm seventy, saying, "Oh, if I'd only run in '04!" I reassured her that wouldn't be the case.

At the outset, a presidential candidate ordinarily has at best a 10 to 15 percent chance of being elected; however, had I run for president, there was a 100 percent certainty I'd miss seeing my children grow up. "I may have another opportunity to run for president," I told her, "and maybe it will make sense then. But the most important thing is that I do right by our kids, because if I don't, *that's* something I'll always regret."

I also felt the honorable thing to do was to make an early decision. I didn't want people committing themselves to my campaign if I wasn't fully committed myself.

I decided to declare my intention not to run on June 15 at a press conference in Indianapolis, where I had the happy job of announcing the federal funding of the Indiana Fatherhood Initiative.

Fortunately, you *can* be a healthy, well-adjusted human being and not run for president of the United States. Maybe I'll make a different decision someday when the boys are older and have their own interests and activities; maybe not. But as I reminded Susan, I was governor of Indiana for eight years, and now I'm a United States senator. I've had wonderful opportunities to serve my state, country, and fellow citizens. I like the sound of applause as much as the next person but hope never to be intoxicated by it. I simply didn't think it was right to put political ambitions ahead of my boys' well-being.

Granted, you don't succeed in politics without a healthy level of ambition—me included—but some things are more important, and your children ought to be one of them.

At the end of the 2000 Congressional session, The Responsible Fatherhood Act expired along with all of the other proposed bills that had failed to become law in the previous two years. I still felt strongly about the bill, though, and I still felt it had a chance of getting passed, so I reintroduced it early in the 2001 session. This time I chose my fellow Hoosier and colleague in the House, Congresswoman Julia Carson, to be the bill's cosponsor. I'd been the first senator to focus on the issue of father absence, but Julia had been promoting fatherhood initiatives in the House before I even arrived in Washington.

Julia has a special interest in the issue because she never knew her own father. She met him only once, when she was four years old, and didn't realize at the time that he was her dad. Growing up in Indianapolis, Julia was too embarrassed to tell the other kids at school that her father wasn't around, so she told them instead that he was a colonel in the U.S. Army, stationed overseas. Of course, she wasn't the only kid at school without a father, but apparently she had the best cover story. By the time she graduated, three other kids were claiming overseas colonel fathers, too.

In 1996, Julia made history by becoming the first woman and the first African American to represent Indianapolis (now Indiana's Seventh District) in Congress. Prior to being elected to Congress, she served eighteen years in the Indiana General Assembly and then six years as Center Township trustee. When Julia first joined the Indiana General Assembly, persons born outside of marriage were referred to in state statute as "illegitimate"—a term that struck her as pejorative. She successfully fought to have it removed from the books and replaced with the term "out of wedlock."

Though I was still optimistic about The Responsible Fatherhood Act, I realized that my best chance to promote responsible fatherhood might end up coming through cosponsorship of a colleague's legislation. One such bill was Senator Olympia Snowe's Strengthening Working Families Act, a bipartisan piece of legislation that included fatherhood initiatives but represented a broader approach to family-strengthening designed to fortify the successful welfare reforms of the previous five years. By focusing on custodial parents, 95 percent of whom are women, that first generation of welfare reform had failed to address the problem of men who bring children into the world and then walk away. It only made sense that those men be a principle focus of the next generation of welfare reform.

The stage was already set for the 2001 Congressional session to be an important one for welfare. The first generation of reform, launched in 1996 by the Personal Responsibility and Work Opportunity Reconciliation Act, was scheduled to expire at the end of the year, and Congress would need to reauthorize that bill or pass a new one. That landmark piece of legislation ended welfare as an entitlement and instead focused on preparing recipients to work. The basic premise underlying the bill was that opportunity, in the form of public support, must go hand in hand with personal responsibility on the part of beneficiaries. At the time the bill was introduced, there was a great hue and cry from people who felt the reforms were unfair, but since then, a consensus has evolved recognizing welfare reform as a success. It's an issue of basic fairness. The vast majority of Americans want government to be compassionate and help people who are down on their luck, but Americans also want to know that welfare recipients are trying to make the most of that helping hand—trying as hard as the working people who pay the taxes that make the helping hand possible.

Much of the debate over welfare reform goes back to a basic philosophical question: What should the role of government be—to guarantee outcomes, or to guarantee opportunity? For me, the answer is some of both, but with an emphasis on the latter. As a society, we want to guarantee certain minimum conditions. Social Security for the elderly, Medicaid for the sick, and welfare for the indigent are examples. As a great nation, America must not countenance our elderly living in dire poverty, our sick dying for want of care, or our poorest children going without food and shelter.

Guaranteeing such basic outcomes is a crucial function of government, but once those thresholds have been met, government's principal focus should be to foster self-sufficiency based on merit and access to opportunity. In doing so, the government essentially says to its citizens, "We're going make sure you have access to the basic building blocks of success—a quality education, health care, decent housing, and so forth—but then it's up to you to make the most of your God-given abilities." This is the bargain implicit in many of the efforts to improve America over the last century, and it's also the thinking behind fatherhood initiatives, which in simplest terms seek to provide decent opportunity for children disadvantaged by the absence of fathers.

Even before Congress passed the first welfare reforms in 1996, those of us in Indiana already knew that the system needed to be changed. As governor, I had signed into law one of the most comprehensive statewide welfare reforms in the nation, making Indiana a leader in bringing people from welfare to work. It all started in 1993, when the state had been on the verge of enacting reform but couldn't because the legislature was gridlocked. The

Republicans wanted tough work requirements, but they weren't willing to provide the necessary resources to enable people to meet them. The Democrats were leery of touching the issue at all; they thought it was unfair to hold welfare recipients to standards of personal accountability.

Since the two parties were at an impasse, I took matters into my own hands. I went to the federal government and used what is called a waiver process to obtain permission to bypass the state legislature and enact experimental welfare reform myself, by executive order. That broke the ice, and the following year, during the 1994 session, we were able to get the law passed by the Indiana General Assembly. By then, I think both the Democrats and Republicans saw that my reform bill used the best of both of their approaches, and they saw that it could work.

As of November 1996, our reform program was expected to achieve more than $140 million in savings over the next six and a half years and move approximately thirty-seven thousand adults to self-sufficiency, reducing the welfare rolls by nearly 50 percent. In 1994, we spent $247.8 million in Indiana on direct welfare payments to families; by the year 2000, we reduced that number by 66 percent, to $83.8 million. The lesson was clear—if you help people find work and dignity, they become self-sufficient, helping themselves and the taxpayers, too.

Julia Carson and I teamed up again that summer to moderate a fatherhood conference at the Thurgood Marshall Center in Washington. The center was a fitting location for a fatherhood conference. The nation's first black YMCA had once been housed in the building, which was designed by African-American architect

William Sidney Pittman and opened in 1908. The Y was originally named after Anthony Bowen, a slave who bought his freedom, moved to Washington, and organized community activities for young African-American men. Over the years, the Bowen Y was frequented by a host of important African Americans, including Charles Drew, inventor of the Blood Bank; poet Langston Hughes; musician Duke Ellington; and basketball great Elgin Baylor. Thurgood Marshall and his mentor, Charles Houston of the Howard University Law School, formulated legal strategies for the civil rights movement there in the 1950s.

Today, the Thurgood Marshall Center is listed on the National Register of Historic Places and houses the Washington chapter of Concerned Black Men. The center is located in D.C.'s predominantly black Shaw neighborhood. Unfortunately, this historically close-knit community is now facing a variety of social problems—including epidemic father absence. And the problem isn't limited to Shaw. The District of Columbia leads the nation in father absence, with no father present in 56 percent of its homes with children.

The conference was hosted by the Democratic Leadership Council, a national group of moderate Democrats who focus on issues that often fall victim to partisan politics. Al From, a native Hoosier who founded the DLC in 1985, describes the organization as an "idea-action network"—we develop ideas, and then put them into action through our work at the federal, state, and local levels. The DLC has always taken a special interest in social policy and played a big role in securing one of the most important anti-poverty efforts of the last three decades: the expansion of the Earned Income Tax Credit, which provides tax relief to America's working poor so that people who work full-time can live above the poverty level. My interest in fatherhood initiatives complemented the DLC's existing commitment to welfare reform, so when I succeeded Joe Lieberman as chairman of the DLC in February, I made fatherhood a top issue and began planning the conference.

For me, the most moving moments of that afternoon were the personal testimonials. During one panel, we heard from DeAndre Davis, a nineteen-year-old high-school dropout, former drug abuser, and expectant father. DeAndre was one of seven children in his family and had never met his own father or even seen his picture. All he knew was his father's name and that he had family in New York City. Now that DeAndre was having a child of his own, he intended to do better than his father had done. At the time of the conference, he was involved with a fatherhood program, working toward his GED (which he subsequently earned), and planning to attend college or join the Air Force.

"If I made the child, I feel like it's my obligation to marry the mother of my child," he told the crowd. "And even if things don't go great with my marriage, I still want to be there 110 percent for my child." The audience interrupted his testimony with applause. "I also promised myself that if I ever had a child, I'd always be there, because I never had a father to come see my basketball games, my football games. He missed out on something great, which is me."

We also heard from Dwayne Grimes, a former drug addict and father of seven. He was fatherless too, having been raised by his grandparents. He knew his dad had lived in Washington, and he told us that as he was driving into town for the conference, he couldn't help scanning the faces of men on the street, hoping for a glimpse of the father he'd never known. When he became addicted to drugs, Dwayne was living with Brenda, the mother of six of his kids. Even though he shared a roof with his children, he says he wasn't much of a father to them because of his addiction. Then one day he realized that his own kids were afraid to come near him. "It

hurt so much," he said. "That's when I understood I needed help."
He decided to get involved with a fatherhood center in Baltimore,
and he credits the center's programs with turning his life around.
He went through detox, married Brenda, and has been clean for
almost four years.

The DLC conference was the first of two events that helped put
fatherhood in the Washington limelight that summer. A few weeks
later, the city hosted the Fourth Annual National Fatherhood
Initiative Summit, which was highlighted by President Bush's
keynote address. Like President Clinton before him, President Bush
has always been very supportive of fatherhood initiatives, and we'd
had occasion to discuss fatherhood issues earlier that year when he
invited about a half-dozen centrist Democrats to the White House.
During his speech, the president graciously acknowledged the work
that Pete Domenici and I have done in promoting fatherhood
initiatives. Striking while the iron was hot, I continued to lobby him
in the following months, urging him to make responsible
fatherhood a keystone of his administration's welfare-reform plan. I
knew that if the president made fatherhood a priority, Congress and
the public would, too.

But then, on September 11, all of Washington's priorities got
rearranged. Following the attacks on the World Trade Center and
the Pentagon, the president and those of us in Congress quickly
made national security our top concern. When it came to my
personal priorities, though, that day didn't rearrange them so much
as reinforce them, reminding me how fortunate I was to have Susan
and the boys in my life at a time when so many fellow Americans
had lost members of their own families.

On the morning of September 11, Susan was in San Diego at a
meeting, I was giving a speech in Washington, and Nick and Beau
were at school. I'll never forget the moment when one of my aides

interrupted the speech to tell me a plane had crashed into the World Trade Center. The whole room fell silent, all of us in a state of horrified disbelief. And then the news got worse. When the second plane hit, we realized the crashes weren't accidents. Already people were worried that Washington would be attacked, too, and forty minutes later, when the Pentagon actually was hit, reports circulated that the White House, State Department and other sites had been struck. Confusion reigned. Nobody knew what was going on.

I was told that the Senate offices were being evacuated and that the Capitol had been closed. I got a phone call from my staff instructing me to go home, and then, about five minutes later, another call telling me *not* to go home—the police were afraid that assassins might be waiting to attack members of Congress at their houses. "Go someplace else," they said.

People were fleeing Washington in droves, and the traffic was terrible. I headed straight for the National Cathedral to get Nick and Beau. I was one of the first parents to arrive. The teachers were just starting to send the children home, and the kids were apprehensive. They knew something bad had happened, but they weren't exactly sure what. Beau spotted me in the pandemonium and ran over. "Dad, what's going on?"

"Some bad men hurt some people," I told him, "but I'm here to make sure you're okay."

We rounded up Nick and went to a neighbor's house, where we stayed that night. The Mandels' son, Alex, goes to school with Nick and Beau, so the boys were able to play while I got down to work. Claudia and Victor were kind enough to let me use a phone and a desk so I could stay in touch with my staff and members of the press, whose demands that day were understandably quite high. After the Russell Building was evacuated, my staff had gone to another building near Capitol Hill and set up an informal office. No contingency plans existed for what Congress should do in such an emergency.

A few hours later, I finally was able to reach Susan. She'd been trying to call me, but the phone lines into Washington were swamped. She was very concerned about the kids and was determined to get home, but the FAA had shut down the airlines earlier in the day. The company she was working for ended up renting a car for her and another board member. They drove across the country nonstop, from San Diego to Washington, in forty-eight hours. Frankly, that was one of the few times I've been really angry with Susan. "Driving across the country is too dangerous," I said. "And I don't want to have to worry about you out in the middle of nowhere." But it turned out she did the right thing, because the airlines didn't start flying again until three days after she got back.

We're lucky the boys were so young at the time of the attacks. Even though we live in Washington, we were able to filter out much of the tragedy. We kept them away from the TV because we didn't want them to see planes crashing into buildings and people jumping out of skyscraper windows. I think it's important for them to know there is such a thing as evil in the world, but I didn't see why five-year-olds should have to face the reality of terrorism and mass murder, nor did I see why terrorists should be allowed to disrupt the lives of young children.

If Nick and Beau had older siblings, or if they'd been even a year or two older, the situation would have been different. They'd have seen the attacks on TV or have heard about them from other kids at school. Nick still had trouble sleeping for a couple of weeks. He's a little more sensitive than his brother, and he knew something was going on. He'd come into our room in the middle of the night and climb into bed with us.

School was cancelled for most of that week, as was the boys' soccer game on Saturday. The following Saturday, however, play

Bayh!
U.S. Senate

Paid for by the Evan Bayh Committee

My campaign poster for the U.S. Senate, May 1998. Six months later, I followed in my father's footsteps, winning the election.

My father, Susan, and the boys joined me onstage after my keynote speech at the 1996 Democratic National Convention in Chicago. The giant hand on the video screen behind us is my own—very surreal.

A proud moment—three generations of Bayhs at my Senate swearing-in. This was the only time the boys were in their little blue suits, but it was worth it.

Making time to have fun with my sons is a priority, as it was on this ski vacation at Beaver Creek, Colorado, in 1999 with Beau (left) and Nick.

A family tradition—each year
we send out Christmas cards
with our family portrait.

resumed. Beau and Nick's team is called the Giants, and at their age their league uses no goalies, which made it easier for the kids to score. I think I enjoyed those games even more than the boys did, watching them have fun, breathing in the crisp autumn mornings, hanging out with the other parents. There was a reporter from *U.S. News & World Report* whose son was on the team, and another parent who worked for *Time*, but we rarely talked politics—just family, soccer, kids.

Before that particular game, the coach gathered the team around and said, "Today's lesson is, 'Don't take the ball away from your teammate.' "

I ribbed him a little. "Coach, we're really starting with the basics, huh?"

"That's right," he said. "You want to know what last week's lesson was? 'Only go in one direction.' "

With the country in such turmoil, I could appreciate the coach's simple approach that day. I turned my attention to the field as Nick and Beau trotted out to their positions.

19
CHALLENGES OF TOMORROW

*I hope that more men will recognize that bringing a
child into the world is not only a tremendous
responsibility, but also a profound opportunity to
help shape the future and make it better.*

AMERICAN FAMILIES ARE facing a host of new and daunting
challenges today. In years past, many families could get by on one
parent's income, allowing the other parent to stay home with the
children. However, economic changes have reduced the number of
high-paying jobs in the United States. As a result, we're seeing more
two-income families and more parents who must work more than
one job. These economic changes have placed families under greater
stress and financial pressure while leaving parents with less time for
their children.

Another great challenge confronting American families is the
coming retirement of the baby boom generation. Our Social
Security system operates on a pay-as-you-go basis, which means that
today's workers pay for the benefits of today's retirees. When Social
Security first started, there were many workers per retiree. However,
by the time we retire and our children are paying our retirement

benefits, there will be only about 2.5 active workers per retiree, meaning our children and grandchildren will have to be much more productive to cover our retirement benefits than we had to be in order to cover our own parents.

Thanks to advances in medicine and health care, those baby boomers will also be living longer lives, thus increasing the chances that they'll outlive their financial resources and be forced to rely on their children for economic support. As a result, members of this "sandwich generation" will increasingly face pressures from two directions at once as they struggle to take care of both their children and their parents.

In addition to these and other challenges, the fatherhood crisis continues to loom as a serious threat to the well-being of American families and our children in particular. Over the past several years, I've come to believe even more deeply in the fight against father absence. The statistics have always been compelling, but the people I've met at fatherhood conferences—fathers, mothers, children— have put a human face on those statistics in a way that motivates me more than mere facts ever could.

It heartens me to see our society working to address some of the emerging challenges facing American families. We're pursuing strong policies for family leave. We're working to ease the burden of retirement for senior citizens, thereby reducing the pressures on their children as well. We're recognizing the importance of quality daycare and educational facilities for the children of single-parent and two-income families.

Unfortunately, when it comes to the fatherhood crisis, our society still isn't paying close enough attention. This is particularly true of our political leadership. It's always easier to deal with the short-term, superficial manifestations of a problem than its long-term, deeper causes.

Our politicians are not immune to basic human psychology. Like the rest of us, they want immediate gratification; they want to be able to show progress and results to their constituents. It's very tempting to just appropriate more money for prisons, anti-drug efforts, educational remediation, and so forth, and say that you've gotten something done than it is to take steps that will actually prevent those problems but won't bear fruit for several years. And therein lies one difficulty of fighting father absence: the fatherhood movement will lead to results, but not before the next election.

A second difficulty involves the very sensitive and personal nature of the problem. When it comes to fighting father absence, elected officials run a great risk of insulting the public if they fail to express themselves in sensitive ways. Men take offense if they feel you're unfairly accusing them of shirking their responsibilities; women take offense if they believe you're failing to value the role that women play in families—especially the role of single women—or if they believe you're adopting a paternalistic view of the world, attempting to roll back the important social progress women have made in the past few decades. On top of that, the fatherhood effort lacks a powerful political lobby, making it hard to compete in a galaxy of more organized constituencies, all of them demanding time, resources, and money. There are, in the end, few clear political benefits for the elected official who decides to champion fatherhood initiatives.

Congress isn't the only guilty party when it comes to ignoring the damage that father absence is doing to our country's children. The silence from the news media is deafening. The media tend to focus on issues that attract ratings, and fatherhood is certainly not a glamorous issue. Understanding the impact of father absence requires more than sound bites, but television in particular doesn't lend itself to the in-depth analysis of such issues. And even when the news media do cover the fatherhood crisis, it's usually a one-time story, not a recurring one, and therefore fails to penetrate the public's consciousness.

Nevertheless, I believe that fatherhood is an issue whose time is near. There will be no "epiphany moment." Rather, the issue will rise in prominence as we come to better understand the challenges we face, until finally the movement will reach a critical mass in which not only opinion leaders, but also public officials, children's rights advocates, and others will come together in recognizing the futility of simply dealing with the symptoms of the problem instead of addressing its underlying causes. I believe that The Responsible Fatherhood Act will eventually be enacted and then built upon in successive years as the growing body of research further demonstrates the ways in which father absence contributes to so many of our social and economic ills. (As this book goes to press, President Bush's budget proposal for the fiscal year 2004 includes $20 million in competitive grants to faith- and community-based organizations, along with Indian tribes and tribal organizations, to encourage and help fathers support their families, avoid welfare, and improve their ability to manage family business affairs.)

As a former governor, however, I don't believe in fighting father absence with a one-size-fits-all, top-down approach. On the contrary, I think the task will require a partnership between the federal and state governments, the public and the private sectors. Since the federal government is already spending huge amounts of money to deal with the manifestations of this problem, I think its role should be in defining what the challenge is, establishing goals for meeting the challenge, and providing resources to states and local governments to implement solutions.

At the same time, the federal government must offer them the flexibility to experiment with how best to meet those goals. What works best in Indiana, for instance, might not be what works best in other states. Finally, the federal government must insist on accountability and demand results. Otherwise, Congress will end up funding programs that don't work, which not only wastes resources but also fuels cynicism about the role of government.

Barely a year after the September 11 attacks, Washington suffered through another nightmare as a pair of snipers terrorized the metropolitan area for more than two weeks, shooting citizens at random. Ten people were murdered and three more were wounded. Children had to be kept inside—no soccer games, no recess on the playground, no Saturday afternoons in the park. At Beau and Nick's school, new security measures were instituted.

The boys were much more aware of what was happening during the killing spree than they had been during the September 11 attacks. Across the country and especially in the Washington area, the story dominated the news and public discourse. Parents and children became even more terrified on the sixth day of the spree, October 7, when a thirteen-year-old boy was shot in the chest and seriously wounded at Benjamin Tasker Middle School in Bowie, Maryland, northeast of Washington.

The country breathed a sigh of relief on October 21 when two men were arrested in connection with the sniper hunt near Richmond, Virginia. Immediately, the public wanted to know more about the suspects. Who could have committed such heinous acts? What in their backgrounds could explain such complete disregard for life? Not surprisingly, both men grew up without fathers. John Allen Muhammad's dad reportedly abandoned the family when Muhammad was very young. John Lee Malvo last lived with his father when he was five or six years old and hasn't seen his father since he was thirteen. Though the majority of fatherless young men grow up to be productive, law-abiding citizens, we cannot ignore the fact that so many of our country's most violent criminals— including almost three-fourths of all long-term prison inmates—are males who grew up without fathers.

In addition to the sadness I felt for the snipers' victims and their families, I was also angry that, in the space of little more than a year, America's children had been subjected to suicidal terrorists crashing airplanes into buildings and madmen with sniper rifles killing citizens at random, apparently without the least bit of remorse. It's a callous world sometimes, a fact that Nick and Beau will soon enough discover for themselves, but I couldn't help feeling that they'd been exposed to it too early.

In the wake of the sniper attacks, the holiday season was especially welcome in our household. The boys were excited to be participating in their first official school play, *The Christmas Story*, which is performed by Beauvoir's first-graders at the National Cathedral each year. Beau received quite an honor when he was picked to play Joseph. Nick, however, was a little disappointed: he'd been offered the more humble role of a shepherd. But then one night when I was reading them *The Christmas Story*, Nick perked up.

"So Dad," he said, "the shepherds got to stay up late, didn't they?"

"I suppose so," I said. "They stayed up waiting for the angel to appear and then went to the manger to look for baby Jesus."

Nick thought this over. "That means they got to stay up almost all night, right? But Joseph, he had to go to bed early in the manger." And that's when Nick decided that being a shepherd was a pretty good role after all. Sometimes the simplest things mean the most to a child.

It's been interesting seeing the world through the eyes of seven-year-olds, an experience I'm savoring one day at a time. Still, I'm looking ahead too, concerned about the world my boys will inherit when they grow up. Twenty years from now, they'll likely be fathers themselves. By that time, my hope for America is that we will have embraced with renewed enthusiasm those enduring values that have always made our country great, one of which is wanting an even better world for our children. That means putting children first, giving our kids the very best opportunity to succeed and fulfill their potential.

I hope more men will recognize that bringing a child into the world is not only a tremendous responsibility, but also a profound opportunity to help shape the future and make it better. There's a saying I'm fond of: "Children are the living messages we send to a time we will not see." It's my hope that those messengers will have good things to say about who and what we are today.

As for Nick and Beau, I want them to be successful in whatever fields of endeavor they choose but understand that a big part of success can never be measured by dollars in the bank or the title that you hold, but rather by the esteem of your friends and the love of your family. I hope, too, that they'll try to give something back to the society they've been blessed to live in.

It's often been said that character is destiny, and I hope Susan and I will have succeeded in teaching them the values and virtues that have always characterized successful people—honesty, kindness, integrity, honor, patriotism, faith. I want them to look back on their childhood and feel that Susan and I gave them a good start in life. I have no doubt that they'll revere their mother. As for me, I hope they'll be able to say that I was a good man who did his best, who loved his family and his country, and who tried to leave both a little better for his having been there.

INDEX